Math: Second Gr

Contents

Introduction

The National Council of Teachers of Mathematics (NCTM) has targeted five content standards in an effort to help students reach their full potential as capable and mathematically competent individuals. The standards include Number and Operations, Algebra, Geometry, Measurement, and Data Analysis and Probability. Within the content standards, NCTM has listed topic standards and expectations for students at all grade levels. *Math* is a series that exposes students to many of the standards as they creatively explore new mathematic ideas and concepts.

Math targets the most important math topics for each grade level. Students gain exposure through hands-on experiences and then have an opportunity to build on this basic knowledge through practice and extension activities. Used as a supplement, *Math* can enhance the mathematical development of all students, no matter what their level of understanding.

Organization and Features

The book consists of five units that focus on the content standards. The 15 lessons in each book are proportional to the grade bands proposed by the NCTM. Each eight-page lesson consists of:

- **Teacher information.** A two-page introduction identifies the targeted standards, materials needed for the lesson, and a description of the activities. To help develop the concepts, the information page identifies **reteaching ideas**, **extension activities**, and suggestions that students can share with family members **at home**. Most importantly, the **answer key** is embedded in these pages to provide easier access between the activity pages and solutions. Finally, information is given about the **Harcourt Achieve website**, where other ideas are just a click away.
- **Manipulatives.** To introduce each concept, the first lesson page is devoted to the use of manipulatives so that students can explore important tenets in a concrete way.
- **Practice.** Follow-up practice is critical to help students transfer concrete understanding to the more abstract math concepts.
- **Extension.** This page allows students another page of practice, but in a more relaxed and inviting format. Students might answer riddles, draw pictures, or follow a code as they continue to practice skill development.
- **Word problems.** Students combine reading comprehension with mathematics as they utilize a variety of problem-solving techniques to answer relevant questions.
- **Enrichment.** The final page in each lesson outlines one or two open-ended activities that require more higher-level, logical, and creative thinking. They are self-directed and require materials available in the classroom.

In addition, each book contains:
- a table of contents that specifies each skill.
- a correlation chart that identifies the specific NCTM expectations by lesson.
- three resource pages to accompany activities.

What Research Says

"Research has solidly established the importance of conceptual understanding in becoming proficient in a subject. When students understand mathematics, they are able to use their knowledge flexibly. . . . Learning the 'basics' is important . . . . In contrast, conceptual understanding enables students to deal with novel problems and settings. They can solve problems that they have not encountered before."

Principles and Standards for School Mathematics: An Overview. 2000. Reston, VA: The National Council of Teachers of Mathematics, Inc.

Correlation to NCTM Standards

CONTENT STRANDS	LESSONS 1	2	3	4	5	6	7	8	9	10	11	12	13	14	15
Number and Operations															
• Count with understanding and recognize "how many" in sets of objects	•	•	•	•	•		•						•	•	
• Use multiple models to develop initial understandings of place value and the base-ten number system		•	•	•	•										
• Develop understanding of the relative position and magnitude of whole numbers and of ordinal and cardinal numbers and their connections	•	•				•									
• Develop a sense of whole numbers and represent and use them in flexible ways, including relating, composing, and decomposing numbers	•	•	•	•	•	•					•		•	•	
• Connect number words and numerals to the quantities they represent, using various physical models and representations	•	•	•	•	•								•		
• Understand various meanings of addition and subtraction of whole numbers and the relationship between the two operations	•		•	•									•		
• Understand the effects of adding and subtracting whole numbers	•		•	•									•		
• Understand situations that entail multiplication and division, such as equal groupings of objects and sharing equally					•										
• Develop and use strategies for whole-number computations, with a focus on addition and subtraction	•		•	•									•		
• Develop fluency with basic number combinations for addition and subtraction	•												•		
• Use a variety of methods and tools to compute, including objects, mental computation, estimation, paper and pencil, and calculators	•		•	•	•								•		
• Understand and represent commonly used fractions, such as $\frac{1}{4}$, $\frac{1}{3}$, and $\frac{1}{2}$										•					
Algebra															
• Sort, classify, and order objects by size, number, and other properties						•	•	•							
• Recognize, describe, and extend patterns such as sequences of sounds and shapes or simple numeric patterns and translate from one representation to another						•									
• Analyze how both repeating and growing patterns are generated						•									
• Illustrate general principles and properties of operations, such as commutativity, using specific numbers					•										
• Model situations that involve the addition and subtraction of whole numbers, using objects, pictures, and symbols	•		•	•											

Correlation to NCTM Standards

CONTENT STRANDS	1	2	3	4	5	6	7	8	9	10	11	12	13	14	15
	LESSONS														
Geometry															
• Recognize, name, build, draw, compare, and sort two- and three-dimensional shapes							•	•	•	•					
• Describe attributes and parts of two- and three-dimensional shapes							•	•	•						
• Investigate and predict the results of putting together and taking apart two- and three-dimensional shapes							•	•	•	•					
• Describe, name, and interpret relative positions in space and apply ideas about relative position							•								
• Recognize and apply slides, flips, and turns							•								
• Recognize and create shapes that have symmetry							•		•						
• Recognize and represent shapes from different perspectives							•	•	•	•					
• Relate ideas in geometry to ideas in number and measurement										•	•				
• Recognize geometric shapes and structures in the environment and specify their location							•	•	•						
Measurement															
• Recognize the attributes of length, volume, weight, area, and time											•	•			
• Compare and order objects according to these attributes											•	•			
• Understand how to measure using nonstandard and standard units											•				
• Measure with multiple copies of units of the same size											•				
• Use tools to measure											•	•			
• Develop common referents for measures to make comparisons and estimates											•	•	•		
Data Analysis and Probability															
• Pose questions and gather data about themselves and their surroundings												•		•	
• Sort and classify objects according to their attributes and organize data about the objects														•	•
• Represent data using concrete objects, pictures, and graphs														•	•
• Describe parts of the data and the set of data as a whole to determine what the data show														•	•
• Discuss events related to students' experiences as likely or unlikely															•
• Apply and adapt a variety of appropriate strategies to solve problems	•	•	•	•	•	•	•	•	•	•	•	•	•	•	•

Lesson 1

Addition and Subtraction to 18

Objectives

- Count with understanding and recognize "how many" in sets of objects
- Develop understanding of the relative position and magnitude of whole numbers and of ordinal and cardinal numbers and their connections
- Develop a sense of whole numbers and represent and use them in flexible ways, including relating, composing, and decomposing numbers
- Connect number words and numerals to the quantities they represent, using various physical models and representations
- Understand various meanings of addition and subtraction of whole numbers and the relationship between the two operations
- Understand the effects of adding and subtracting whole numbers
- Develop and use strategies for whole-number computations, with a focus on addition and subtraction
- Develop fluency with basic number combinations for addition and subtraction
- Use a variety of methods and tools to compute, including objects, mental computation, estimation, paper and pencil, and calculators
- Model situations that involve the addition and subtraction of whole numbers, using objects, pictures, and symbols
- Apply and adapt a variety of appropriate strategies to solve problems

Vocabulary

addition—joining one thing to another

difference—the answer when a pair of numbers is subtracted

fact family—the group of addition and subtraction sentences that use the same three numbers

subtraction—taking one thing away from another

sum—the answer when two or more numbers are added together

Materials

- pencils, number cubes, dominoes with numbers to 9, craft paper (optional), marker (optional), blue and red connecting cubes (optional), bi-colored counters (optional), plastic cups (optional), index cards (optional), construction paper (optional), large self-stick notes (optional), tape (optional)

Lesson Pages

Page 8 **(Manipulatives)**
Using a number line, children practice adding and subtracting facts to 18.

Page 9 **(Practice)**
Children practice addition facts.

Page 10 **(Practice)**
Children practice subtraction facts.

Page 11 **(Extension)**
Children add and subtract and use the answers to draw a shape.

Page 12 **(Word Problems)**
Children write number sentences and solve them.

Page 13 **(Enrichment)**
Activity Card 1: Partners roll a number cube and write an addition sentence using the numbers.

Activity Card 2: To develop an understanding of fact families, children choose 3 dominoes and write the fact family for each pair of numbers on each domino.

Another Look

- Draw a large number line on craft paper. Call out number sentences that children model by hopping along the number line. (Visual, Kinesthetic, Auditory, ELL)
- Give partners 9 each of blue and red connecting cubes. Call out a number from 10–18. Have one partner use some red and some blue cubes to make a cube train. Challenge the other partner to say 2 addition and 2 subtraction sentences to show the fact family. Then have partners switch roles to show the same number in different ways. (Visual, Kinesthetic, Auditory, ELL)

Extension

- Place from 11–18 bi-color counters in plastic cups. Have partners get a cup and empty it. Ask them to write the fact family for the number of cubes in that cup. Have partners repeat the activity several times.
- Write numbers 1–9 on cards. On construction paper, write facts to 18. Cover one number in each fact with a self-stick note. Then tape the facts to the walls at children's eye level in different parts of the room. Pass out the cards and have children stand by the fact that their card completes.

At Home

- Tell children to gather 18 of one item, such as pennies, buttons, or beans. Have them ask a family member to remove 1–9 of the items so that children can say the subtraction sentence.
- Using the same items above, tell children to choose some of the items. Have them ask a family member to choose more. Challenge the child to say an addition sentence to tell how many in all.

- Visit www.harcourtachieve.com/achievementzone for additional ideas and activity pages.

Answer Key

Page 8

1. 11 **2.** 14
3. 12 **4.** 12
5. 18 **6.** 9
7. 7 **8.** 9
9. 6 **10.** 6

Page 9

1. 11 **2.** 16
3. 14 **4.** 12
5. 11 **6.** 14
7. 18 **8.** 13
9. 13 **10.** 11
11. 12 **12.** 14
13. 13 **14.** 12
15. 12

Page 10

1. 9 **2.** 4
3. 9 **4.** 9
5. 7 **6.** 7
7. 7 **8.** 6
9. 7 **10.** 9
11. 8 **12.** 9
13. 5 **14.** 8
15. 7

Page 11

1. 6 **2.** 12
3. 15 **4.** 9
5. 6 **6.** 14
7. 16 **8.** 8
9. 15 **10.** 12
11. 16
Shape: cube

Page 12

1. $7 + 4 = 11$
2. $12 - 5 = 7$
3. $18 - 9 = 9$
4. $8 + 6 = 14$

Page 13

Answers will vary.

Name ______________________ Date ______________

USING A NUMBER LINE

Hop in Line

Add. Use the number line. The first one is done for you.

1. 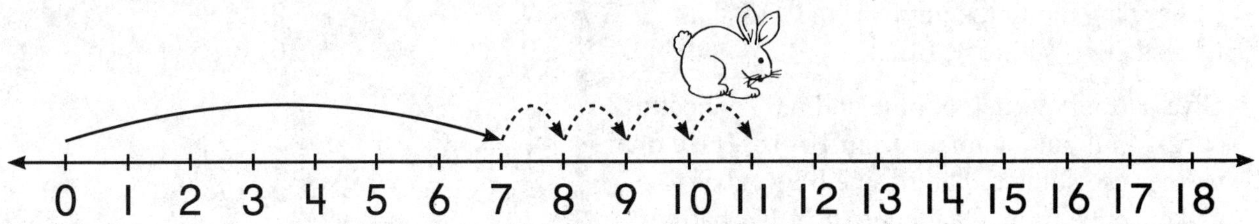

7 + 4 = ______

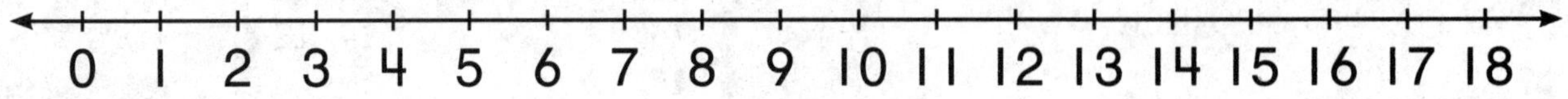

2. 6 + 8 = ______ **3.** 3 + 9 = ______

4. 5 + 7 = ______ **5.** 9 + 9 = ______

Subtract. Use the number line. The first one is done for you.

6. 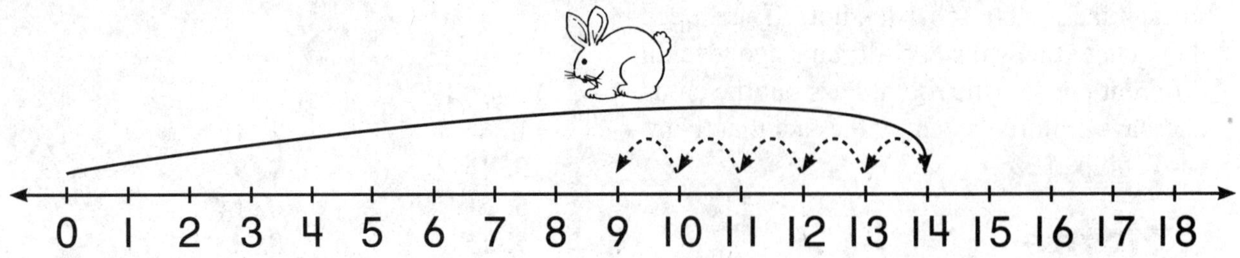

14 − 5 = ______

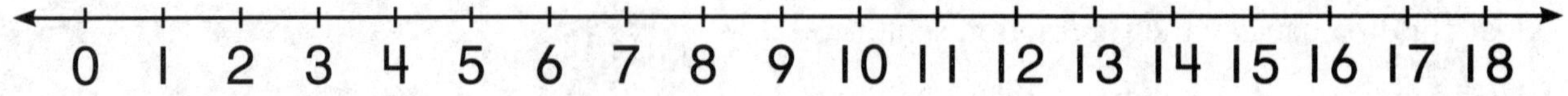

7. 11 − 4 = ______ **8.** 17 − 8 = ______

9. 15 − 9 = ______ **10.** 13 − 7 = ______

Name ______________________ Date ______________

PRACTICING ADDITION FACTS

Dino-mite Sums

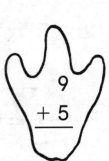

Add.

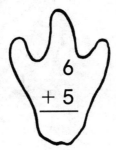

1. $6 + 5$
2. $8 + 8$
3. $9 + 5$
4. $3 + 9$
5. $7 + 4$
6. $8 + 6$
7. $9 + 9$
8. $6 + 7$
9. $8 + 5$
10. $9 + 2$
11. $4 + 8$
12. $7 + 7$
13. $9 + 4$
14. $6 + 6$
15. $7 + 5$

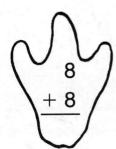

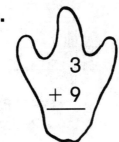

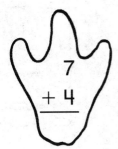

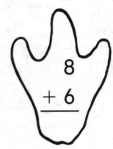

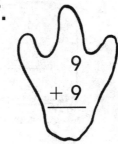

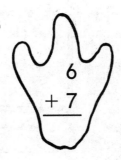

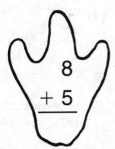

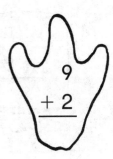

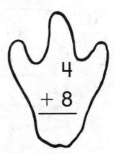

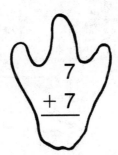

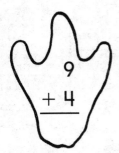

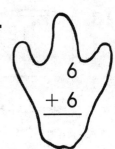

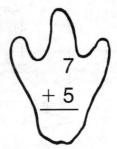

Name ______________________ Date ______________

PRACTICING SUBTRACTION FACTS

The Penguin Difference

Subtract.

1. $12 - 3 =$ ___
2. $13 - 9 =$ ___
3. $15 - 6 =$ ___
4. $17 - 8 =$ ___
5. $14 - 7 =$ ___
6. $11 - 4 =$ ___
7. $16 - 9 =$ ___
8. $11 - 5 =$ ___
9. $15 - 8 =$ ___
10. $18 - 9 =$ ___
11. $14 - 6 =$ ___
12. $17 - 8 =$ ___
13. $12 - 7 =$ ___
14. $16 - 8 =$ ___
15. $13 - 6 =$ ___

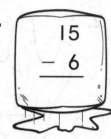

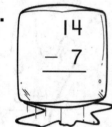

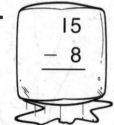

Name ____________________ Date ____________

ADDING AND SUBTRACTING FACTS

Brushing Up on Addition and Subtraction

Add or subtract.

1.	14 − 8	**2.**	6 + 6	**3.**	7 + 8				
4.	18 − 9	**5.**	13 − 7	**6.**	7 + 7				
7.	8 + 8	**8.**	15 − 7	**9.**	9 + 6	**10.**	8 + 4	**11.**	9 + 7

What did the artist paint? Connect the dots to find out. Begin with the answer to the first problem and continue with the answers to the rest of the problems.

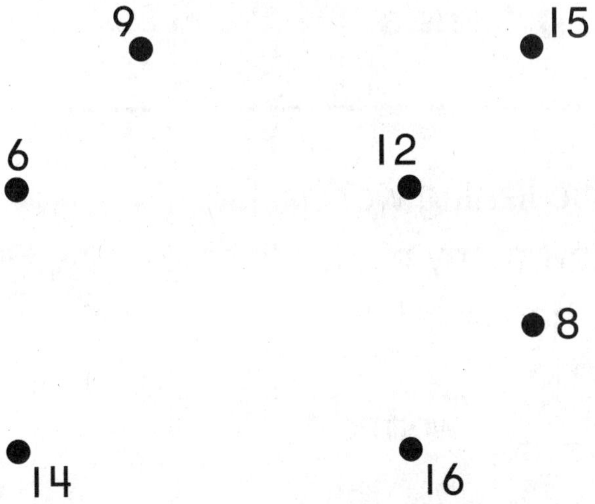

Name ______________________ Date ____________

SOLVING WORD PROBLEMS

Fishing for Answers

Write a number sentence and solve.

1. Lee fished for 7 hours on Saturday. He fished for 4 hours on Sunday. How many hours did Lee fish in all?

_____ ◯ _____ = _____ hours

2. Rita catches 12 fish. She lets 5 fish go because they are too small. How many fish does Rita keep?

_____ ◯ _____ = _____ fish

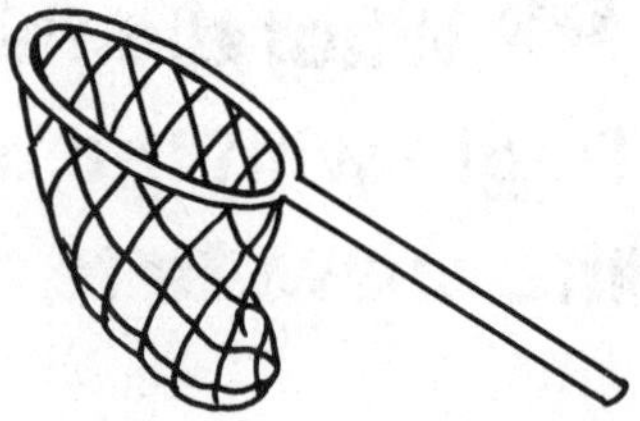

3. A store has 18 fishing nets. It sells 9 nets. How many nets are left?

_____ ◯ _____ = _____ nets

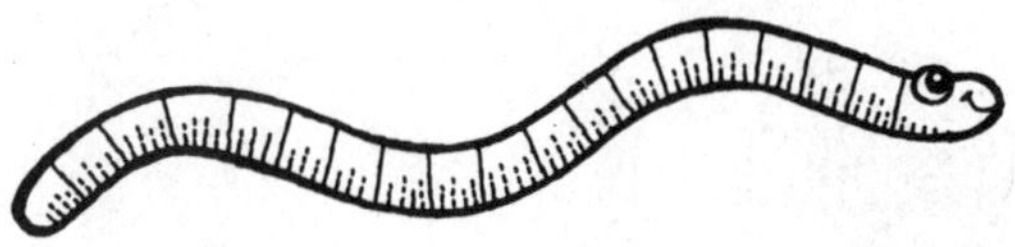

4. Dan has 8 plastic fishing worms. He buys 6 more. How many plastic fishing worms does he have in all?

_____ ◯ _____ = _____ worms

Name ______________________ Date ____________

Writing Facts

➔ Work with a partner. Each of you rolls a number cube. Write the addition sentence. Roll the cubes 4 times in all.

Name ______________________ Date ____________

Identifying Fact Families

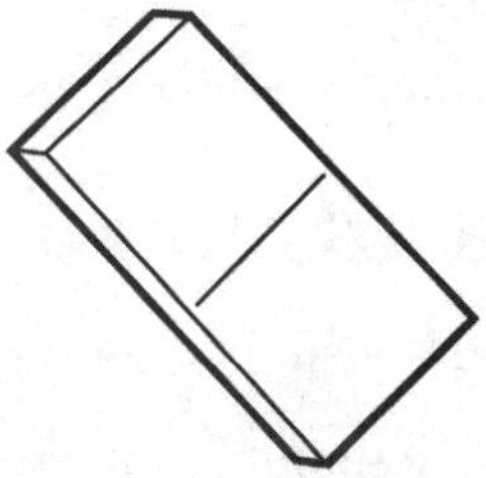

➔ Choose 3 dominoes. Draw the dots on the dominoes below. Write the fact family for each.

1. 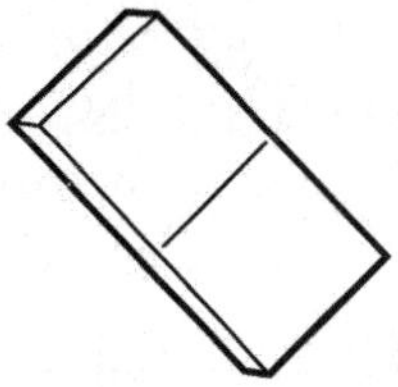

___ ○ ___ = ___

___ ○ ___ = ___

___ ○ ___ = ___

___ ○ ___ = ___

2. 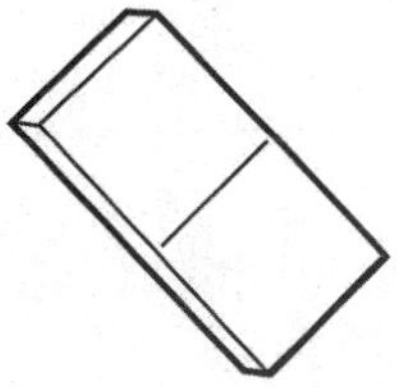

___ ○ ___ = ___

___ ○ ___ = ___

___ ○ ___ = ___

___ ○ ___ = ___

3. 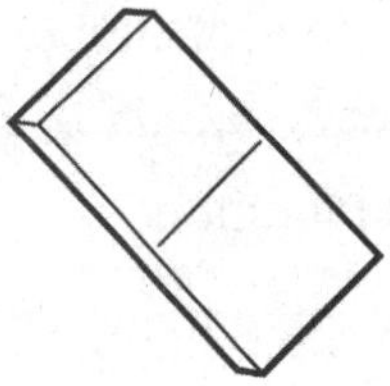

___ ○ ___ = ___

___ ○ ___ = ___

___ ○ ___ = ___

___ ○ ___ = ___

Lesson 2

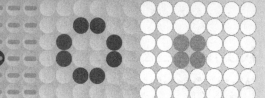

Place Value: Numbers to 1,000

Objectives

- Count with understanding and recognize "how many" in sets of objects
- Use multiple models to develop initial understandings of place value and the base-ten number system
- Develop understanding of the relative position and magnitude of whole numbers and of ordinal and cardinal numbers and their connections
- Develop a sense of whole numbers and represent and use them in flexible ways, including relating, composing, and decomposing numbers
- Connect number words and numerals to the quantities they represent, using various physical models and representations
- Apply and adapt a variety of appropriate strategies to solve problems

Vocabulary

cube—a single block that represents ones

flat—a manipulative made with 100 joined blocks that represents hundreds

place value—the value of a digit based on its placement in a number

rod—a manipulative made with 10 stacked cubes that represents tens

Materials

- flats, rods, cubes, crayons, pencils, Place-Value Chart (page 126), number cubes, paper (optional)

Lesson Pages

Page 16 **(Manipulatives)**
Children use flats and rods to model groups of tens and hundreds on the place-value chart found on page 126. Then they color to show their models and write how many in all on page 16.

Page 17 **(Practice)**
After counting groups of manipulatives, children write how many hundreds, tens, and ones in a chart and how many in all.

Page 18 **(Practice)**
Children circle the value for an underlined digit in numbers.

Page 19 **(Extension)**
Children complete two dot-to-dot pictures and identify the rule to complete them.

Page 20 **(Word Problems)**
Children read stories and solve them.

Page 21 **(Enrichment)**
Activity Card 1: Children roll 3 number cubes and find all the ways to show the number. Then they choose one and list all the ways to write the number.

Activity Card 2: Children try to figure out Paul's favorite number from clues. The clues narrow the choices to four numbers. Children write the last clue.

Another Look

- Have children color the headings in the Place-Value Chart (page 126) to match the colors of the manipulatives. If the flats are yellow, have them color the heading in the chart yellow. Then call out numbers for them to model. (Visual, Kinesthetic, Auditory, ELL)
- Call out 3-digit numbers that end in 9. Have partners use flats, rods, and cubes to model the number. Then have them add one more cube and name the new number. Lead them to discover that they must trade the 10 cubes for a rod. Repeat the process, counting by tens and having children practice trading rods for flats.

Extension

- Ask children to create number patterns using 3-digit numbers. Then have children work with partners to identify the pattern and extend it.
- Ask children to write number riddles. Have them write a 3-digit number on paper. Then have them write three clues about the number on the back of the paper. Clues can include place value, greater or less than, or skip-count information. Children trade papers to solve the riddles.

At Home

- Ask children to look at the number of pages in 5 magazines and books. Have them write the titles and numbers of pages on paper. Then have them order the numbers of pages from least to greatest.
- Tell children to take a walk with a family member. Ask them to look for numbers on streets, mailboxes, and houses. Have them discuss if each number is greater than or less than the number they noticed before.
- Visit www.harcourtachieve.com/achievementzone for additional ideas and activity pages.

Answer Key

Page 16
1. 20
2. 70
3. 300
4. 600

Page 17
1. 543
2. 487
3. 615
4. 399
5. 730
6. 605
7. 999

Page 18
1. 7 tens
2. 4 hundreds
3. 6 ones
4. 1 hundred
5. 0 ones
6. 3 tens

Page 19
Check that children connect the dots to show a ship and a train.
1. add 1
2. add 10

Page 20
1. 500
2. 229, 230, 231
3. 420
4. less than

Page 21
Card 1: Answers will vary.
Card 2: Possible numbers for the given clues: 29, 47, 65, 83. The final clue and number will vary.

Name ______________________ Date ______________

UNDERSTANDING TENS AND HUNDREDS

Group Together

Use rods and the place-value chart. Show how many. Color to show the number. Write how many in all.

1. 2 groups of 10 __20__

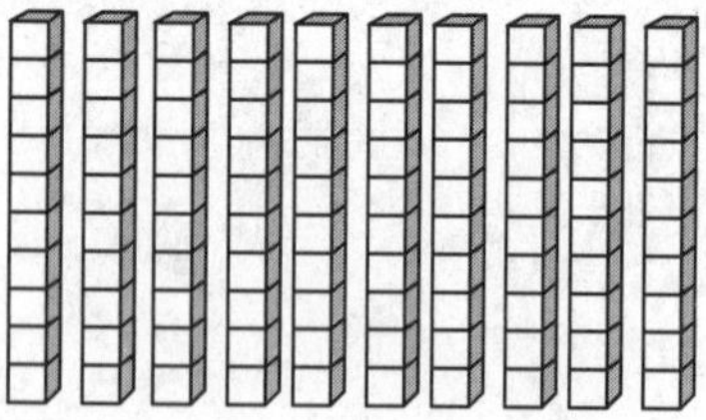

2. 7 groups of 10 ______

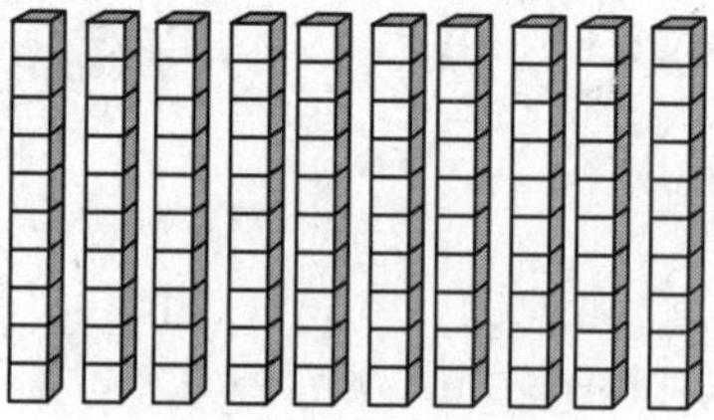

Use flats. Show how many. Color to show the number. Write how many in all.

3. 3 groups of 100 ______

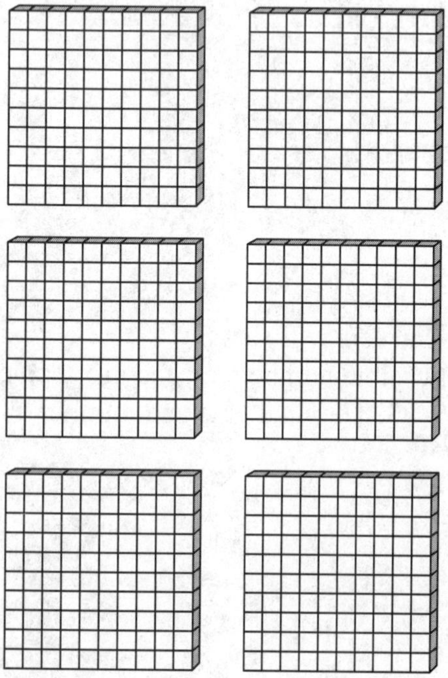

4. 6 groups of 100 ______

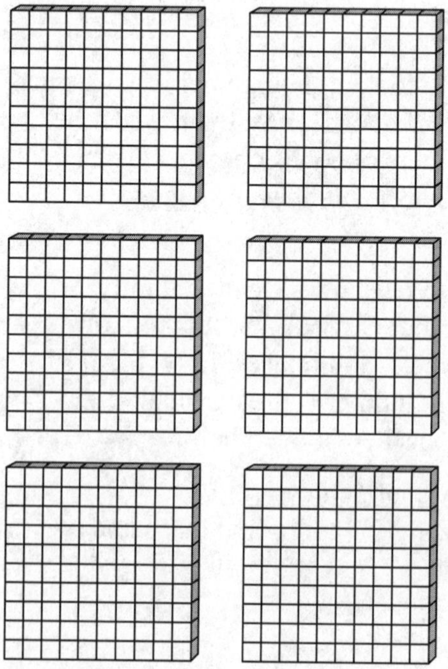

Name ______________________ Date ______________

WRITING NUMBERS

On the Chart

Write how many on the chart. Then write the number.

1.

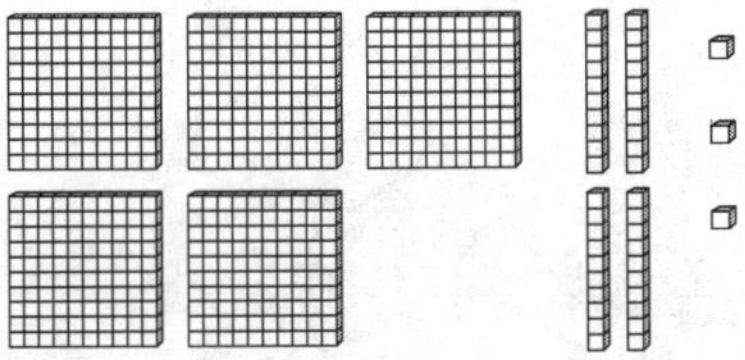

hundreds	tens	ones

______

2.

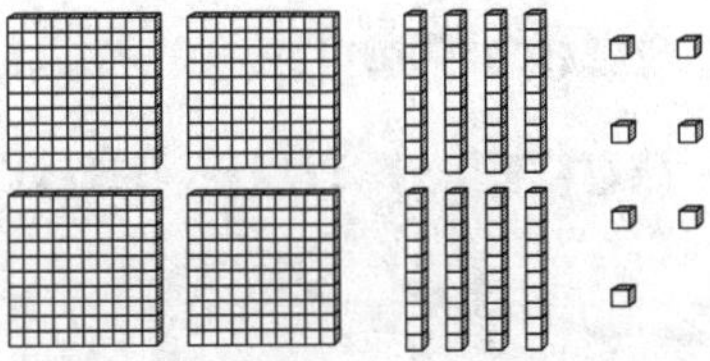

hundreds	tens	ones

______

3.

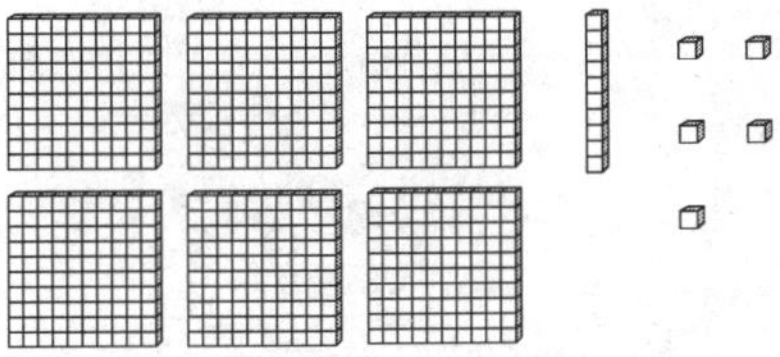

hundreds	tens	ones

______

4.

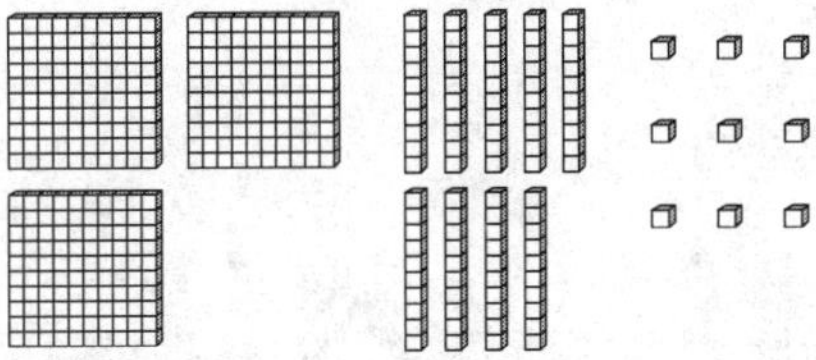

hundreds	tens	ones

______

5.

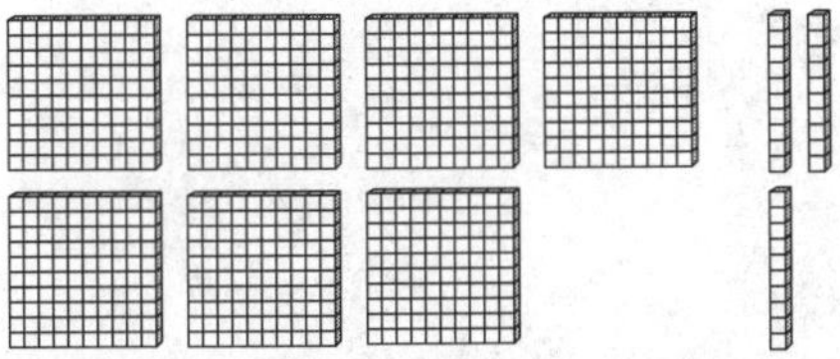

hundreds	tens	ones

______

6.

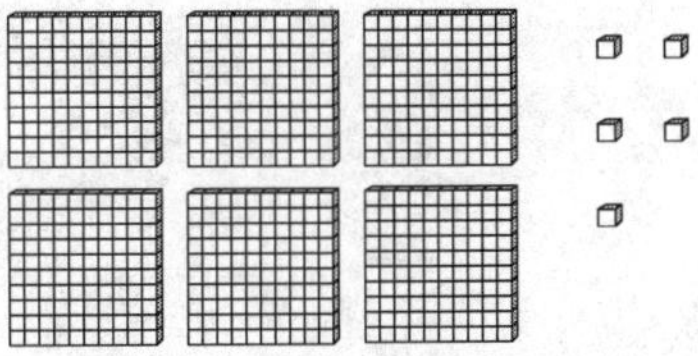

hundreds	tens	ones

______

7.

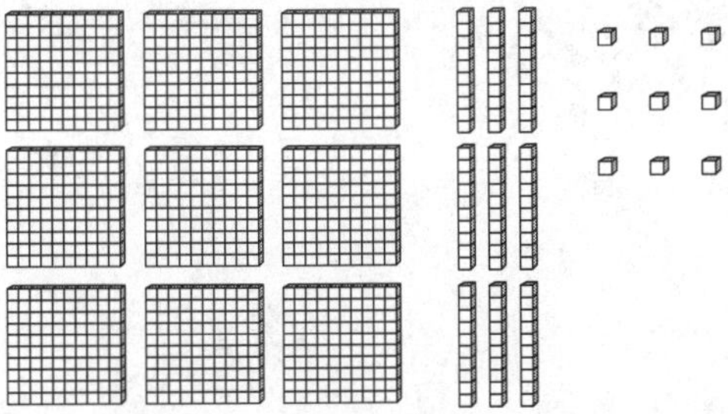

hundreds	tens	ones

______

Name ____________________ Date ____________

IDENTIFYING PLACE VALUE

Monkeying Around with Numbers

Look at each number. Circle the place value of the number that is underlined.

1.

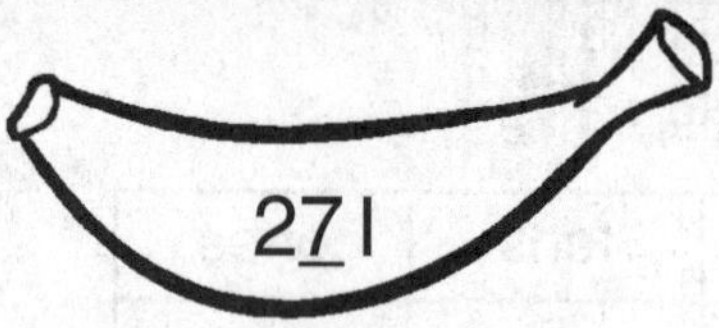

7 hundreds

7 tens

7 ones

2.

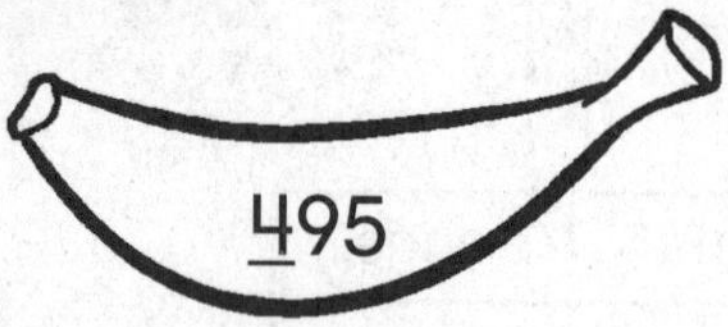

4 hundreds

4 tens

4 ones

3.

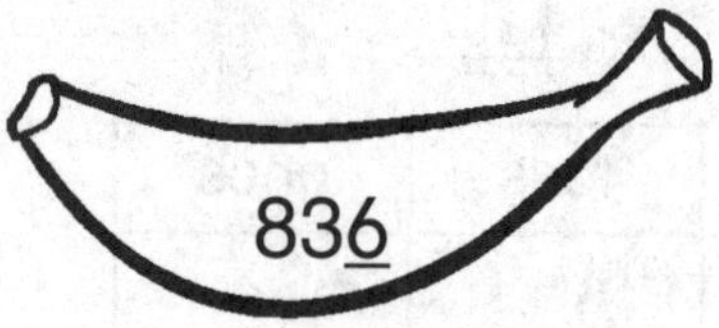

6 hundreds

6 tens

6 ones

4.

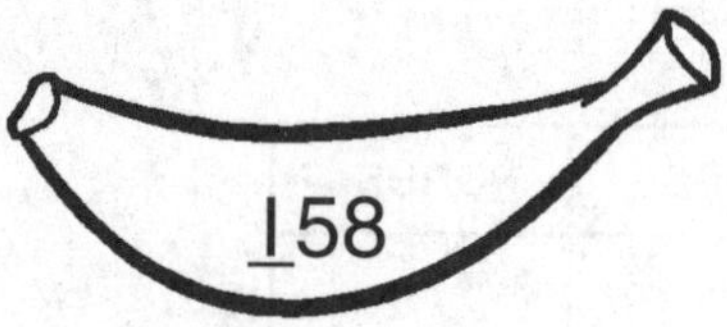

1 hundred

1 ten

1 one

5.

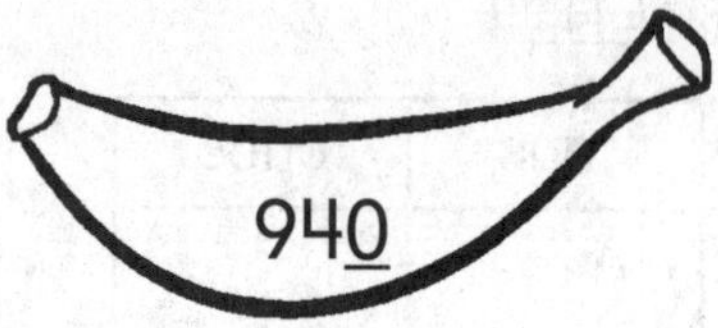

0 hundreds

0 tens

0 ones

6.

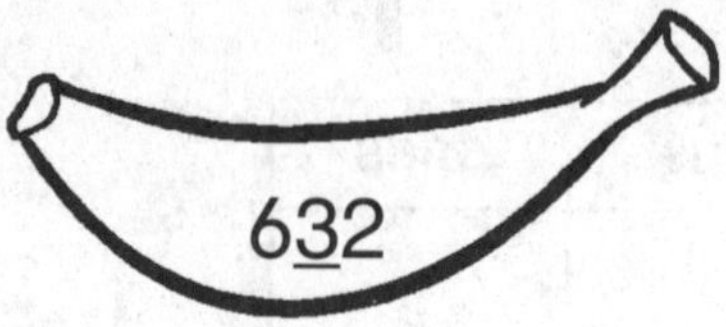

3 hundreds

3 tens

3 ones

Name ______________________ Date ______________

ORDERING NUMBERS

Picture Perfect

Connect the dots in order. Start at 100. What is the rule? Write it.

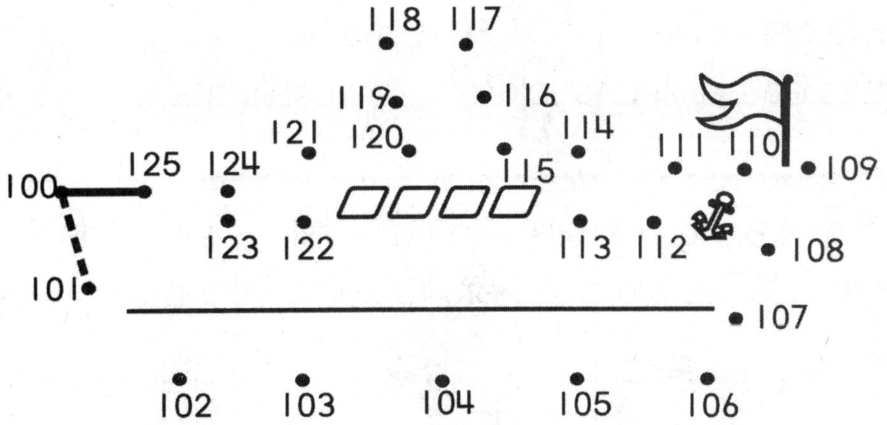

1. Rule: ______________________

Connect the dots in order. Start at 150. What is the rule? Write it.

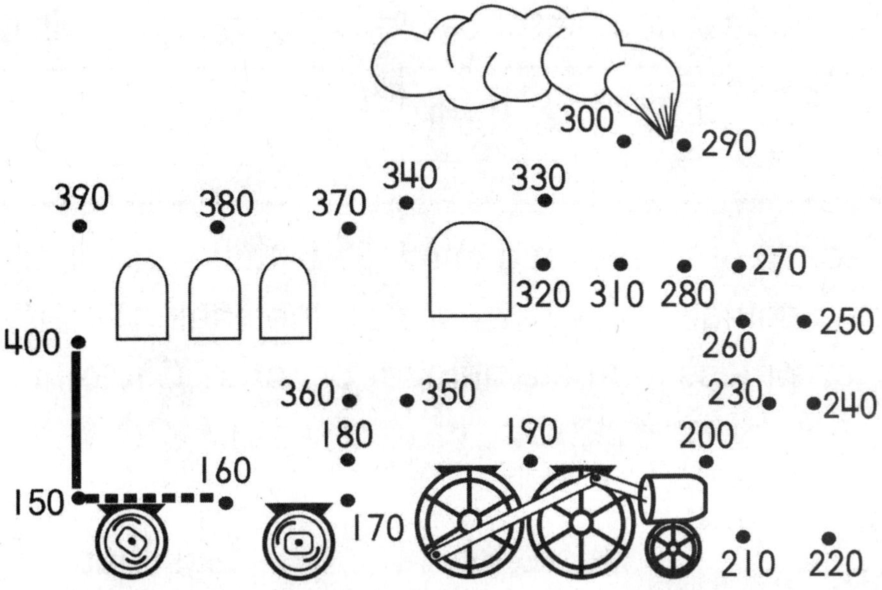

2. Rule: ______________________

Name ____________________ Date ____________

SOLVING WORD PROBLEMS

Store Stories

Read each story. Solve.

1. Bill unpacks 5 boxes of flashlights. There are 100 flashlights in each box. How many flashlights does Bill unpack? _____ flashlights

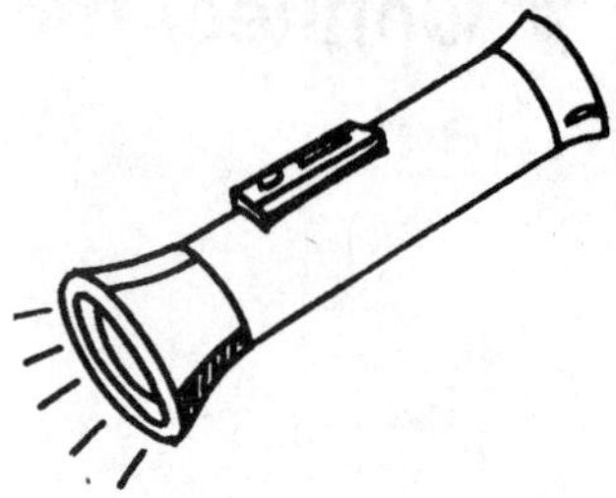

2. There are 228 jugs of milk in a case. Mr. Luna adds 3 more jugs to the case. Write the numbers to show how many jugs he has in the case.

3. Len is making a sign. He has these number cards. He wants to make the largest number possible. What number will Len put on the sign?

0	2	4

[ ]

4. Kim needs to put cans on a shelf. She thinks the shelf holds 378 cans. She actually puts 387 cans on the shelf. Was Kim's guess more than or less than the number of cans? Circle the answer.

more than   less than

Name ______________________________ Date ______________

Naming Numbers

➜ Roll 3 number cubes. Write the numbers on the cubes below. How many numbers can you make using all 3 numbers? Write them on the lines.

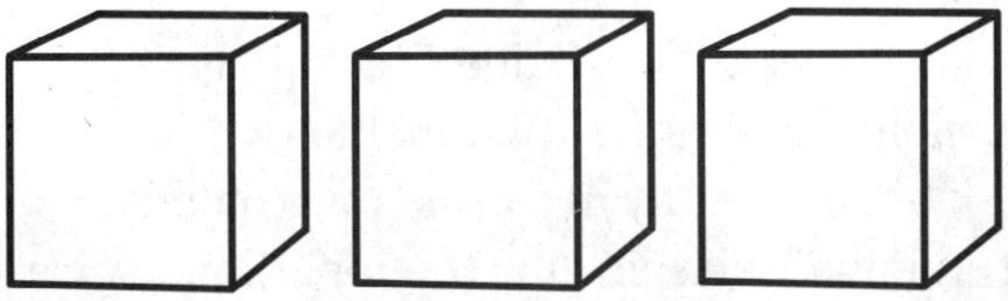

____ ____ ____ ____ ____ ____

➜ Choose 1 number from above. Circle it. How many ways can you write it? Use another piece of paper if you need to.

Name ______________________________ Date ______________

Writing a Number Riddle

➜ Paul has a favorite number. How many numbers fit all the clues? Write them.

- It is an odd number.
- It has 2 digits.
- Its digits equal 11.

➜ Write 1 more clue that tells about Paul's favorite number. Give the clue to a friend. Ask the friend to guess the number.

Lesson 3

2-Digit Addition with Regrouping

Objectives

- Count with understanding and recognize "how many" in sets of objects
- Use multiple models to develop initial understandings of place value and the base-ten number system
- Develop a sense of whole numbers and represent and use them in flexible ways, including relating, composing, and decomposing numbers
- Connect number words and numerals to the quantities they represent, using various physical models and representations
- Understand various meanings of addition and subtraction of whole numbers and the relationship between the two operations
- Understand the effects of adding and subtracting whole numbers
- Develop and use strategies for whole-number computations, with a focus on addition and subtraction
- Use a variety of methods and tools to compute, including objects, mental computation, estimation, paper and pencil, and calculators
- Model situations that involve the addition and subtraction of whole numbers, using objects, pictures, and symbols
- Apply and adapt a variety of appropriate strategies to solve problems

Vocabulary

addend—a number added to another number

regrouping—exchanging 10 ones for 1 ten or vice versa

Materials

- rods, cubes, Place-Value Chart (page 126), pencils, ten frames (optional), counters (optional), penny and dime manipulatives (optional), plastic cups (optional), index cards (optional)

Lesson Pages

Page 24 **(Manipulatives)**
Partners use rods and cubes on a place-value chart to add numbers in an algorithm.

Page 25 **(Practice)**
Using place-value charts, children practice 2-digit addition with regrouping.

Page 26 **(Practice)**
Children practice 2-digit addition with regrouping without place-value charts.

Page 27 **(Extension)**
Children add algorithms and use the sums to complete a puzzle.

Page 28 **(Word Problems)**
Children read stories and solve them.

Page 29 **(Enrichment)**
Activity Card 1: Children make at least 4 lists of bakery goods that they can buy with 60¢.
Activity Card 2: In this activity, children add numbers in a chart to find a path in which the sum is 29.

Another Look

- Provide counters and ten frames. Write 2-digit addition sentences on the board. Help children decide if they should regroup or not based on the counters in the ten frame. (Visual, Kinesthetic, ELL)
- Put dimes and pennies in plastic cups. Have children count the amounts and trade for the smallest number of coins. Then have them work with a partner to add the two amounts. (Kinesthetic, Visual)

Extension

- Invite children to make their own number puzzle similar to the one on page 27.
- Have children write their birth date on cards. Then say a 2-digit number. Challenge children to find a partner with a card whose date, when added together, is close to that number.

At Home

- Ask children to record the number of pages they read each day for a week. Then have them add the numbers and find the sum.
- Suggest children look at food ads in the newspaper. Challenge them to find two items whose prices are close to $1.00 when purchased together. Ask them to cut out the items, glue them on paper, and write the addition sentence.
- Visit www.harcourtachieve.com/achievementzone for additional ideas and activity pages.

Answer Key

Page 24

1. 2 tens, 12 ones; yes; 3 tens, 2 ones; 32
2. 3 tens, 17 ones; yes; 4 tens, 7 ones; 47

Page 25

1. 33 **2.** 50
3. 31 **4.** 62
5. 31 **6.** 63
7. 62 **8.** 72

Page 26

1. 47 **2.** 83
3. 85 **4.** 79
5. 63 **6.** 65
7. 52 **8.** 44
9. 82 **10.** 76
11. 51 **12.** 62
13. 62 **14.** 55

Page 27
Across
1. 61 **2.** 93
3. 76 **4.** 97
5. 92
Down
1. 68 **3.** 77
4. 95 **5.** 91

Page 28

1. 48
2. 25
3. 43 + 39 = 82
4. 23 + 28 = 51

Page 29
Card 1: Answers will vary.
Card 2: Answers will vary.
One path is: 7, 9, 2, 4, 6, 1.

Name ______________________ Date ____________

UNDERSTANDING 2-DIGIT ADDITION WITH REGROUPING

Trading Ten

Use rods and cubes. Add. Regroup if you need to.

tens	ones

1.

tens	ones
1	
2	7
+	5
3	2

Add. Write how many. 2 tens 12 ones

Can you make a ten? (yes) no

Write how many now. 3 tens 2 ones

← Write the sum.

2.

tens	ones
☐	
3	9
+	8

Add. Write how many. ____ tens ____ ones

Can you make a ten? yes no

Write how many now. ____ tens ____ ones

← Write the sum.

Name ______________________ Date ______________

PRACTICING ADDITION WITH REGROUPING

The Trading Game

Add. Regroup if you need to.

1.

tens	ones
□	
2	5
+	8

2.

tens	ones
□	
4	3
+	7

3.

tens	ones
□	
2	9
+	2

4.

tens	ones
□	
5	6
+	6

5.

tens	ones
□	
2	3
+	8

6.

tens	ones
□	
4	5
+ 1	8

7.

tens	ones
□	
3	3
+ 2	9

8.

tens	ones
□	
5	7
+ 1	5

Name ______________________________ Date ______________

PRACTICING ADDITION WITH REGROUPING

"Sum" Baseball Fun

Add. Regroup if you need to.

1. $\begin{array}{r} 19 \\ + 28 \\ \hline \end{array}$

2. $\begin{array}{r} 57 \\ + 26 \\ \hline \end{array}$

3. $\begin{array}{r} 78 \\ + 7 \\ \hline \end{array}$

4. $\begin{array}{r} 62 \\ + 17 \\ \hline \end{array}$

5. $\begin{array}{r} 47 \\ + 16 \\ \hline \end{array}$

6. $\begin{array}{r} 28 \\ + 37 \\ \hline \end{array}$

7. $\begin{array}{r} 29 \\ + 23 \\ \hline \end{array}$

8. $\begin{array}{r} 17 \\ + 27 \\ \hline \end{array}$

9. $\begin{array}{r} 6 \\ + 76 \\ \hline \end{array}$

10. $\begin{array}{r} 68 \\ + 8 \\ \hline \end{array}$

11. $\begin{array}{r} 24 \\ + 27 \\ \hline \end{array}$

12. $\begin{array}{r} 37 \\ + 25 \\ \hline \end{array}$

13. $\begin{array}{r} 58 \\ + 4 \\ \hline \end{array}$

14. $\begin{array}{r} 19 \\ + 36 \\ \hline \end{array}$

Name ______________________ Date ______________

PRACTICING ADDITION WITH REGROUPING

Puzzled with Addition

Add. Use the answers to complete the puzzle.

Across

1.
```
   1
  42
+ 19
----
  61
```

2.
```
  71
+ 22
----
```

3.
```
  58
+ 18
----
```

4.
```
  92
+  5
----
```

5.
```
  77
+ 15
----
```

Down

1.
```
  19
+ 49
----
```

3.
```
  29
+ 48
----
```

4.
```
  64
+ 31
----
```

5.
```
  37
+ 54
----
```

1. 6	1	■	■	2.	
	■	3.		■	■
■	4.		■	5.	
■		■	■		■

Name ______________________ Date ______________

SOLVING WORD PROBLEMS

Carrot Crazy

Read each story. Solve.

1. Mr. Carlos is selling carrots. He sells them in groups of tens and as ones. How many carrots does Mr. Carlos have in his store?

____ carrots

2. Sal is making carrot cake. He has 5 carrots at home. He goes to the store to buy more carrots. He buys 2 groups of ten. How many carrots does Sal have now?

____ carrots

3. Lee is making a carrot salad. She has 4 tens and 3 ones. She buys 3 more tens and 9 more ones. How many carrots does she have in all?

____ ◯ ____ = ____ carrots

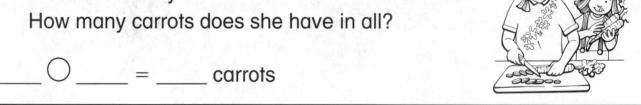

4. David makes carrot muffins for a bake sale. He bakes 23 muffins in the morning. He bakes 28 muffins in the afternoon. How many muffins does David bake in all?

____ ◯ ____ = ____ muffins

Name ______________________________ Date ______________

Making a List

➜ You have 60¢. What can you buy? Make 4 lists on another piece of paper.

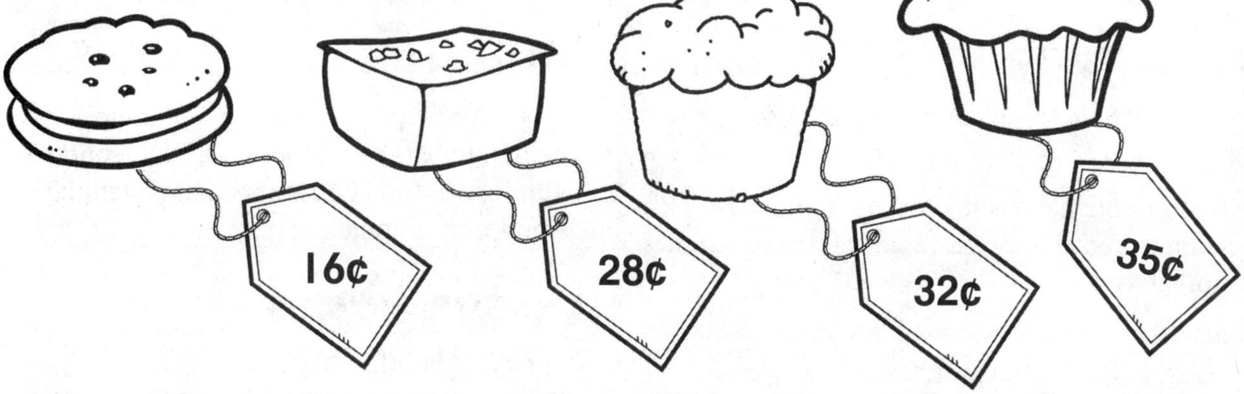

Name ______________________________ Date ______________

Adding Along the Path

➜ Find a path in which the sum is 29. You can start at any square. You can move up and down. You can move left and right.

8	4	2
1	6	9
5	3	7

Lesson 4

2-Digit Subtraction with Regrouping

Objectives

- Count with understanding and recognize "how many" in sets of objects
- Use multiple models to develop initial understandings of place value and the base-ten number system
- Develop a sense of whole numbers and represent and use them in flexible ways, including relating, composing, and decomposing numbers
- Connect number words and numerals to the quantities they represent, using various physical models and representations
- Understand various meanings of addition and subtraction of whole numbers and the relationship between the two operations
- Understand the effects of adding and subtracting whole numbers
- Develop and use strategies for whole-number computations, with a focus on addition and subtraction
- Use a variety of methods and tools to compute, including objects, mental computation, estimation, paper and pencil, and calculators
- Model situations that involve the addition and subtraction of whole numbers, using objects, pictures, and symbols
- Apply and adapt a variety of appropriate strategies to solve problems

Vocabulary

checking—using an inverse operation to find if the answer is correct

Materials

- rods, cubes, pencils, crayons, dominoes with numbers to 9 (optional), food coupons (optional), food containers that match the coupons (optional)

Lesson Pages

Page 32 **(Manipulatives)**
Partners use rods and cubes on a place-value chart to subtract numbers in an algorithm.

Page 33 **(Practice)**
Children practice 2-digit subtraction with regrouping.

Page 34 **(Practice)**
Children develop an understanding that addition and subtraction are inverse operations when they check subtraction problems.

Page 35 **(Extension)**
Children color a picture according to a code of the number of tens in differences.

Page 36 **(Word Problems)**
Children read stories and solve them.

Page 37 **(Enrichment)**
Activity Card 1: Children plan the activities for a 90-minute birthday party.
Activity Card 2: Students subtract pairs of numbers in a subtracting square that equal a given difference.

Another Look

- Provide rods and cubes. Have children build numbers you name. Then have them determine the number of each manipulative when trading 1 ten for 10 ones. (Kinesthetic, Visual, Auditory, ELL)
- Give partners 10 rods and 10 cubes. Point out that 10 rods equal 100. Tell children that they will subtract numbers you name. Then call out numbers from 1–9. Children work together to trade 1 ten for 10 ones and find the difference. Continue until the difference is 0. (Visual, Kinesthetic, Auditory, ELL)

Extension

- Provide dominoes with numbers to 9. Then have partners take turns selecting a domino. They use the dots to make 2 pairs of numbers and write 4 subtraction sentences.
- Gather food coupons and the containers and prices for those foods. Have children find the cost of each food when the coupons are redeemed.

At Home

- Have children ask a family member to record the time it takes for children to complete each activity in preparation for bed. Have children add the times to find how long they take in all.
- Invite children to use the dates on a calendar to write and solve subtraction problems to share with the class.
- Visit www.harcourtachieve.com/achievementzone for additional ideas and activity pages.

Answer Key

Page 32

1. no; yes; 1 ten, 11 ones; 1 ten, 6 ones; 16
2. no; yes; 3 tens, 12 ones; 3 tens, 4 ones; 34

Page 33

1. 49	**2.** 38
3. 29	**4.** 31
5. 36	**6.** 75
7. 26	**8.** 12
9. 28	**10.** 72
11. 19	**12.** 55
13. 22	**14.** 19

Page 34

1. 55; 55 + 12 = 67
2. 39; 39 + 48 = 87
3. 6; 6 + 77 = 83
4. 15; 15 + 30 = 45
5. 33; 33 + 21 = 54
6. 29; 29 + 32 = 61
7. 52; 52 + 28 = 80
8. 17; 17 + 55 = 72
9. 58; 58 + 41 = 99
10. 4; 4 + 58 = 62

Page 35

Check children's answers and colors.

Page 36

1. 45 − 8 = 37	**2.** 84¢ − 50¢ = 34¢
3. 96 − 17 = 79	**4.** 26 − 19 = 7

Page 37

Card 1: Answers will vary.

Card 2:

26			
71	78	52	15
75	49	96	79
42	63	37	53
16	37	41	15

Name ______________________ Date ____________

UNDERSTANDING 2-DIGIT SUBTRACTION WITH REGROUPING

Trading Ten

Use rods and cubes. Subtract. Regroup if you need to.

tens	ones

1.

tens	ones
1	
~~2~~	1
−	5
1	6

Can you subtract? yes (no)

Should you regroup? (yes) no

Write how many tens and ones. 1 tens 11 ones

Subtract. Write how many now. 1 tens 6 ones

← Write the difference.

2.

tens	ones
☐	
4	2
−	8

Can you subtract? yes no

Should you regroup? yes no

Write how many tens and ones. ____ tens ____ ones

Subtract. Write how many now. ____ tens ____ ones

← Write the difference.

Name ______________________________ Date ________________

PRACTICING SUBTRACTION WITH REGROUPING

Cheesy Subtraction

➜ **Subtract. Regroup if you need to.**

1. $\begin{array}{r} 52 \\ -\ 3 \\ \hline \end{array}$

2. $\begin{array}{r} 46 \\ -\ 8 \\ \hline \end{array}$

3. $\begin{array}{r} 38 \\ -\ 9 \\ \hline \end{array}$

4. $\begin{array}{r} 38 \\ -\ 7 \\ \hline \end{array}$

5. $\begin{array}{r} 42 \\ -\ 6 \\ \hline \end{array}$

6. $\begin{array}{r} 84 \\ -\ 9 \\ \hline \end{array}$

7. $\begin{array}{r} 65 \\ -\ 39 \\ \hline \end{array}$

8. $\begin{array}{r} 29 \\ -\ 17 \\ \hline \end{array}$

9. $\begin{array}{r} 54 \\ -\ 26 \\ \hline \end{array}$

10. $\begin{array}{r} 99 \\ -\ 27 \\ \hline \end{array}$

11. $\begin{array}{r} 60 \\ -\ 41 \\ \hline \end{array}$

12. $\begin{array}{r} 75 \\ -\ 20 \\ \hline \end{array}$

13. $\begin{array}{r} 58 \\ -\ 36 \\ \hline \end{array}$

14. $\begin{array}{r} 88 \\ -\ 69 \\ \hline \end{array}$

Name ______________________ Date ____________

CHECKING SUBTRACTION

CheCKing Out

Subtract. Then check by adding.

1.
```
  67     55
- 12   + 12
----   ----
  55     67
```

2.
```
  87   ____
- 48   ____
----
       ____
```

3.
```
  83   ____
- 77   ____
----
       ____
```

4.
```
  45   ____
- 30   ____
----
       ____
```

5.
```
  54   ____
- 21   ____
----
       ____
```

6.
```
  61   ____
- 32   ____
----
       ____
```

7.
```
  80   ____
- 28   ____
----
       ____
```

8.
```
  72   ____
- 55   ____
----
       ____
```

9.
```
  99   ____
- 41   ____
----
       ____
```

10.
```
  62   ____
- 58   ____
----
       ____
```

Name ______________________ Date ____________

IDENTIFYING TENS

Pay Attention to the Colors

Subtract. How many tens are in your answer? Find the color for that many tens. Use it to color that part of the picture.

0 tens—brown	3 tens—purple
1 ten—orange	4 tens—green
2 tens—gray	5 tens—blue

Name ______________________________ Date ______________

SOLVING WORD PROBLEMS

Riding on the Subway

Read each story. Solve.

1. There are 45 people on the subway. At one stop, 8 people get off. How many people are still on the subway?

_____ ◯ _____ = _____ people

2. Luis has 84¢. He buys a subway ticket for 50¢. How much money does Luis have left?

_____¢ ◯ _____¢ = _____¢

3. Yuki has a book with 96 pages. She reads 17 pages on the subway. How many pages does she have left to read?

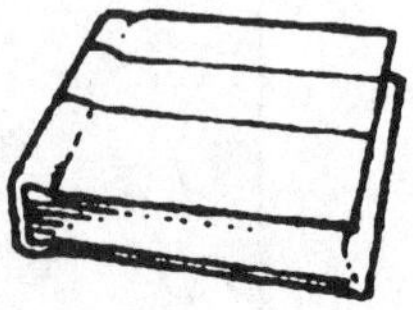

_____ ◯ _____ = _____ pages

4. Rhonda lives 26 miles from the subway station. She has driven 19 miles already. How many more miles does Rhonda need to drive before she gets to the station?

_____ ◯ _____ = _____ miles

Name ________________________ Date ______________

Planning a Party

Imagine that your birthday is next week. Your mother says that you can have a party. It will be from 2:00 to 3:30, which is 90 minutes long. What will you do? How long will each activity last? Plan your party.

____

____

____

____

Name ________________________ Date ______________

Subtracting Square

Subtract the numbers that are next to each other. Which pairs equal the top number? Circle them.

26			
71	78	52	15
75	49	96	79
42	63	37	53
16	37	41	15

Multiplication

Objectives

- Count with understanding and recognize "how many" in sets of objects
- Use multiple models to develop initial understandings of place value and the base-ten number system
- Develop a sense of whole numbers and represent and use them in flexible ways, including relating, composing, and decomposing numbers
- Connect number words and numerals to the quantities they represent, using various physical models and representations
- Understand situations that entail multiplication and division, such as equal groupings of objects and sharing equally
- Use a variety of methods and tools to compute, including objects, mental computation, estimation, paper and pencil, and calculators
- Illustrate general principles and properties of operations, such as commutativity, using specific numbers
- Apply and adapt a variety of appropriate strategies to solve problems

Vocabulary

factor—a number that is multiplied by another number

product—the answer when two or more numbers are multiplied together

Materials

- counters, pencils, crayons, dried beans, craft paper (optional), marker (optional), connecting cubes (optional), containers (optional), food recipe (optional), 1-inch graph paper (optional), self-sealing plastic bags (optional)

Lesson Pages

Page 40 **(Manipulatives)**
Using counters to represent balls, children relate multiplication to repeated addition.

Page 41 **(Practice)**
Children count groups of birds to solve multiplication sentences.

Page 42 **(Practice)**
To develop an understanding of the Commutative Property of Multiplication, children complete number sentences and draw lines between the related facts.

Page 43 **(Extension)**
Children find the missing numbers in algorithms to solve a riddle.

Page 44 **(Word Problems)**
Children read stories and solve.

Page 45 **(Enrichment)**
Activity Card 1: In this activity, children find all the multiplication sentences in which the product is 12.
Activity Card 2: Children color blocks in a quilt and write multiplication sentences to show the color groups.

Another Look

- Draw a large number line with numbers 0–20 on craft paper. Call out a repeated addition fact and have volunteers jump along the line to show the number sentence. The other children in the group say the skip numbers as the volunteer jumps. Help children identify the corresponding multiplication fact. (Visual, Kinesthetic, Auditory, ELL)

- Make trains in groups of 2, 3, 4, and 5 cubes. Put different numbers of trains in containers. Have children identify both the addition and multiplication sentences that the containers show. (Visual, Kinesthetic, Auditory, ELL)

Extension

- Write a simple recipe on the board. Have children double and triple the recipe to find the ingredient amounts.
- Give children 1-inch graph paper. Invite them to look at the design on Card 2 on page 45. Challenge them to make a color design of their own. Have partners trade designs and write the multiplication sentences to show the colors and patterns.

At Home

- Send home with children a small, self-sealing bag of dried beans. Suggest that they use the beans as manipulatives to show multiplication facts. Have them write the multiplication sentences for the facts they make.
- Challenge children to go on a multiplication hunt to find items in the house that come in groups, such as crayons, eggs, shoes, and table settings for dinner.
- Visit www.harcourtachieve.com/achievementzone for additional ideas and activity pages.

Answer Key

Page 40
1. 2, 4; 2; 2, 4
2. 2, 6; 3; 3, 6
3. 3, 6; 2; 2, 6
4. 3, 9; 3; 3, 9

Page 41
1. 3; 2; 6
2. 4; 2; 8
3. 4; 3; 12
4. 2; 4; 8

Page 42
1. $2 \times 4 = 8$; line to $4 \times 2 = 8$
2. $3 \times 5 = 15$; line to $5 \times 3 = 15$
3. $4 \times 3 = 12$; line to $3 \times 4 = 12$
4. $2 \times 6 = 12$; line to $6 \times 2 = 12$

Page 43
1. 6; line to $3 \times 2 = 6$
2. 10; line to $2 \times 5 = 10$
3. 12; line to $4 \times 3 = 12$
4. 18; $3 \times 6 = 18$
5. 8; $2 \times 4 = 8$
Riddle: POPCORN

Page 44
1. Children draw 4 balloons in each hand.; $2 \times 4 = 8$ or $4 \times 2 = 8$
2. Possible answers: $2 + 2 + 2 + 2 + 2 + 2 = 12$; $6 \times 2 = 12$; $2 \times 6 = 12$
3. $3 \times 3 = 9$
4. 21; 3×7

Page 45
Card 1: Possible answers: 1×12; 12×1; 2×6; 6×2; 3×4; 4×3
Card 2: Check that children color the blocks correctly.
red: $4 \times 4 = 16$
blue: $4 \times 1 = 4$
green: $4 \times 1 = 4$
yellow: $4 \times 2 = 8$

Name ______________________ Date ____________

EXPLORING MULTIPLICATION

Balls of Fun

Put 2 counters on each seal's nose. Trace the counters. Count the groups of 2.

1.

2 + 2 = 4

2 groups of 2

2 × 2 = 4

2.

____ + 2 + 2 = ____

____ groups of 2

____ × 2 = ____

Put 3 counters on each seal's nose. Trace the counters. Count the groups of 3.

3.

____ + 3 = 6

____ groups of 3

____ × 3 = 6

4.

____ + 3 + 3 = ____

____ groups of 3

____ × 3 = ____

Name ______________________ Date ____________

PRACTICING MULTIPLICATION

Bird Count

Answer the questions. Then multiply.

1. 

How many groups? ____

How many birds in each group? ____

3 × 2 = ____

2. 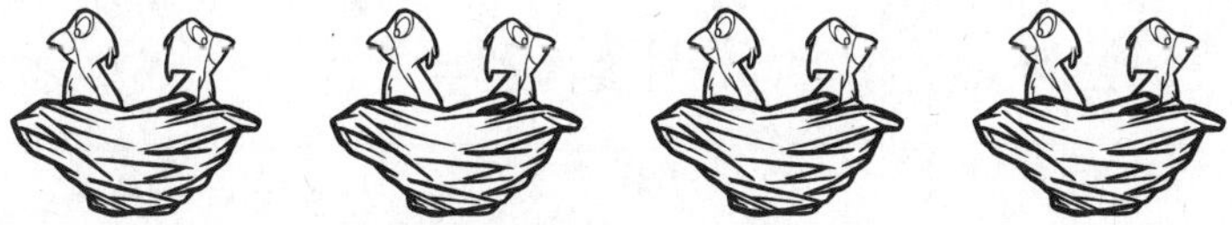

How many groups? ____

How many birds in each group? ____

4 × 2 = ____

3. 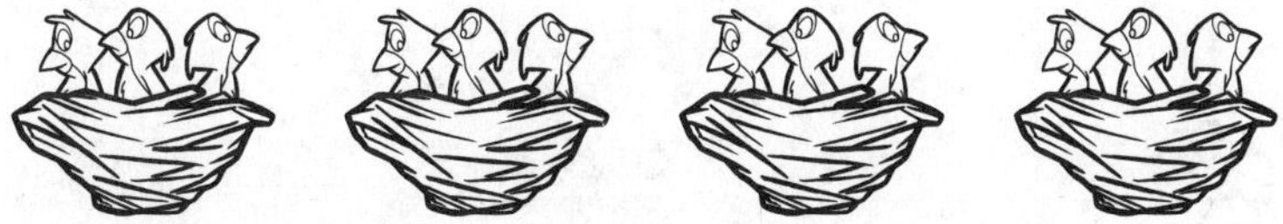

How many groups? ____

How many birds in each group? ____

4 × 3 = ____

4. 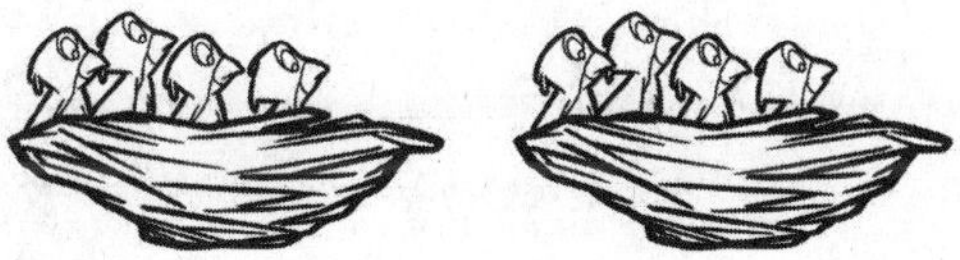

How many groups? ____

How many birds in each group? ____

2 × 4 = ____

Name ______________________ Date ____________

UNDERSTANDING THE COMMUTATIVE PROPERTY OF MULTIPLICATION

Flower Times

Complete each multiplication sentence. Then draw a line to the matching facts.

1. 

____ × ____ = ____

groups flowers

2. 

____ × ____ = ____

groups flowers

3. 

____ × ____ = ____

groups flowers

4. 

____ × ____ = ____

groups flowers

5 × 3 = ____

4 × 2 = ____

6 × 2 = ____

3 × 4 = ____

Name ______________________ Date ______________

RELATING ADDITION AND MULTIPLICATION

Corny Riddles

Complete the number sentences. Draw lines to the matching sentences.

1. 2 + 2 + 2 = ____	2 × 5 = ____ (O)
2. 5 + 5 = ____	2 × 4 = ____ (N)
3. 3 + 3 + 3 + 3 = ____	3 × 2 = ____ (P)
4. 6 + 6 + 6 = ____	3 × 6 = ____ (R)
5. 4 + 4 = ____	4 × 3 = ____ (C)

Write the letter code that matches the problem number to solve the riddle.

What did the baby corn call his father?

____	____	____	____	____	____	____
1	2	1	3	2	4	5

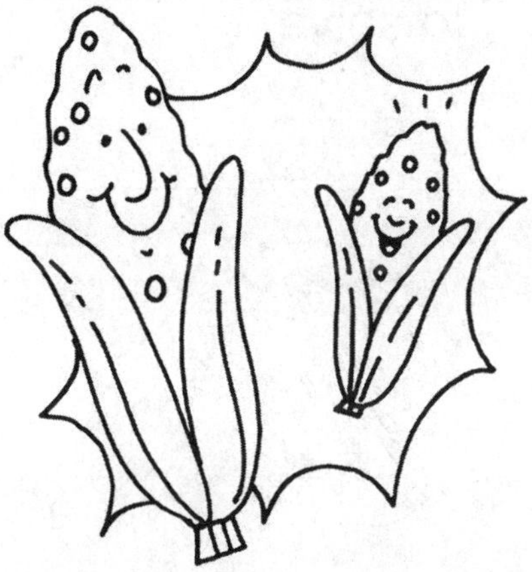

Name ______________________ Date ____________

SOLVING WORD PROBLEMS

Clown Time Problems

Read each story. Solve.

1. The clown has 4 balloons in each hand. How many balloons does the clown have? Draw a picture. Then write the multiplication sentence to solve.

____ ◯ ____ = ____

2. The clown has 6 pairs of shoes. Write 3 number sentences to show how many shoes the clown has.

____

____

____

3. The clown has 3 shirts. There are 3 buttons on each shirt. How many buttons does the clown have in all? Write a multiplication sentence to solve.

____ ◯ ____ = ____

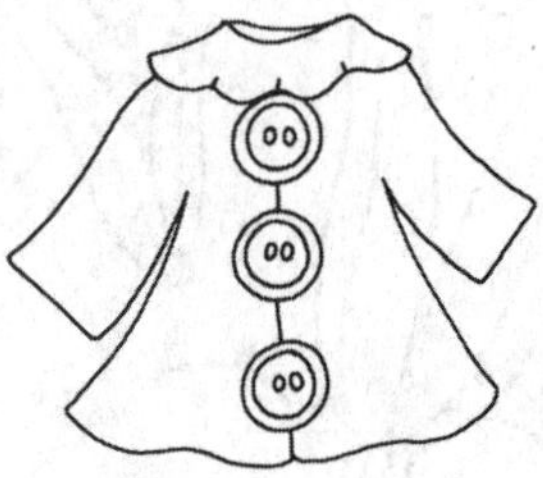

4. The clown is in the circus show 3 times each day for one week. The clown writes a multiplication sentence to find out how many times he is in the show. Complete the number sentence. What is another way that the clown can show the sentence? Circle it.

$7 \times 3 =$ ____

1×7 $\qquad$ $7 + 1$

$7 + 3$ $\qquad$ 3×7

Name ____________________ Date ____________

Designing Bean Pictures

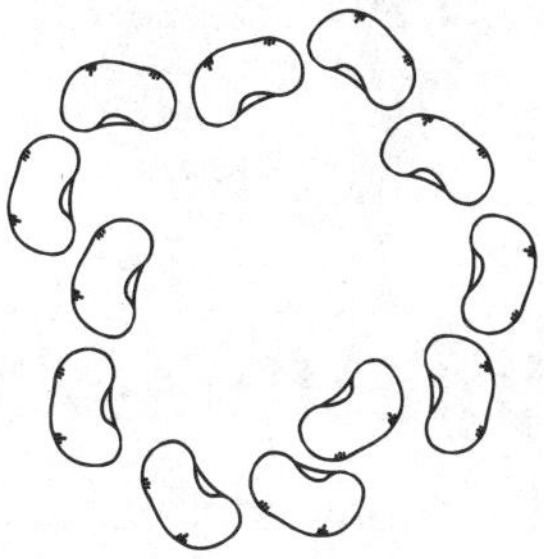

Get 12 beans. How many different ways can you arrange all 12 beans to show multiplication sentences? Circle the beans to show the groups. Then write each multiplication sentence.

1.  ____ × ____ = 12
2.  ____ × ____ = 12
3.  ____ × ____ = 12
4.  ____ × ____ = 12
5.  ____ × ____ = 12
6.  ____ × ____ = 12

Name ____________________ Date ____________

Coloring Patterns

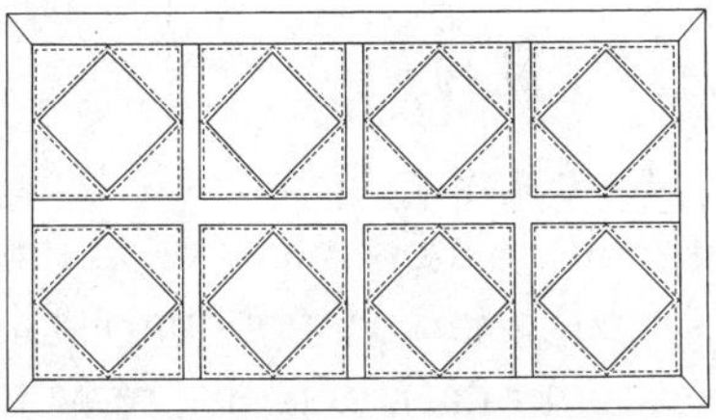

Ana made a quilt. Color the blocks to show the design. Write multiplication sentences to show how many blocks of each color Ana used.

R = red B = blue
G = green Y = yellow

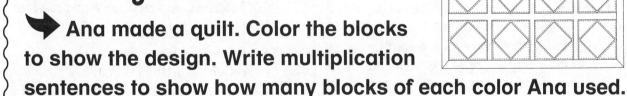

R	R	B	G	R	R	B	G
R	R	Y	Y	R	R	Y	Y
Y	Y	R	R	Y	Y	R	R
B	G	R	R	B	G	R	R

red: ____ × ____ = ____

blue: ____ × ____ = ____

green: ____ × ____ = ____

yellow: ____ × ____ = ____

Lesson 6

Patterns

Objectives

- Develop understanding of the relative position and magnitude of whole numbers and of ordinal and cardinal numbers and their connections
- Develop a sense of whole numbers and represent and use them in flexible ways, including relating, composing, and decomposing numbers
- Sort, classify, and order objects by size, number, and other properties
- Recognize, describe, and extend patterns such as sequences of sounds and shapes or simple numeric patterns and translate from one representation to another
- Analyze how both repeating and growing patterns are generated
- Apply and adapt a variety of appropriate strategies to solve problems

Materials

- bi-color counters, pencils, connecting cubes (optional), pattern blocks (optional), craft paper (optional), marker (optional), 1-inch graph paper (optional), crayons, recycled wallpaper books or fabric (optional), self-sealing plastic bags (optional), several kinds of dried beans (optional)

Lesson Pages

Page 48 **(Manipulatives)**
Children use bi-color counters to make three different color patterns to show the paths that Red Riding Hood could take to Grandma's house. Encourage more than just an AB pattern. Extend the activity to include more colors (using connecting cubes), shape patterns (using pattern blocks), and number patterns.

Page 49 **(Practice)**
Children complete geometric patterns and identify the rule.

Page 50 **(Practice)**
Children complete number patterns and identify the skip-count rule.

Page 51 **(Extension)**
Children complete 5 different dot-to-dot pictures in a farm scene.

Page 52 **(Word Problems)**
Children complete a table and use it to solve word problems.

Page 53 **(Enrichment)**
Activity Card: Children look for 3 different number patterns in a 100s chart.

Another Look

- Use pattern blocks to build shape patterns. Have partners work together to describe and extend the pattern. (Visual, Kinesthetic, Auditory, ELL)

- Draw a large number line with numbers 0–50 on craft paper. Help children learn skip-count patterns as they jump to the numbers. (Visual, Kinesthetic, Auditory, ELL)

Extension

- Provide 1-inch graph paper. Have children complete an addition table for numbers 0–9. Have them color each doubles sum blue. Have them color each doubles plus 1 sum yellow. Encourage them to discuss the patterns they see.
- Display several sheets of wallpaper from recycled books or patterned fabric squares. Invite children to describe the color and shape patterns they see.

At Home

- Send home self-sealing bags with two kinds of dried beans. Have children use the beans to make patterns and describe them. Suggest that they get a family member to make patterns that the children can extend and describe.
- Ask children to go on a pattern hunt for numbers. Ask them to take a walk with a family member and look for number patterns on mailboxes, houses, and streets.
- Visit www.harcourtachieve.com/achievementzone for additional ideas and activity pages.

Answer Key

Page 48
Answers will vary.

Page 49
1. circle; rectangle; Rule: 1 rectangle followed by 1 circle.
2. rectangle; arrow; Rule: 2 arrows followed by 1 rectangle.
3. square; oval; Rule: 2 squares followed by 2 ovals.
4. star; Rule: 1 star followed by 2 triangles.
5. rectangle; rectangle; Rule: 1 circle followed by 1 rectangle.

Page 50
1. 30; 35; 45; 50; 60; Rule: Count by fives.
2. 24; 26; 30; 32; 36; 38; Rule: Count by twos.
3. 10; 20; 40; 50; 70; 80; Rule: Count by tens.
4. 18; 21; 27; 30; 36; 39; Rule: Count by threes.

Page 51
Check that children connect the dots to show a tree, barn, pond, henhouse, and frog.

Page 52
1. 50¢
2. 40¢
3. 70¢
4. 6
5. 10¢
6. 8

Page 53
Answers will vary.

Name ______________________________ Date ______________

IDENTIFYING PATTERNS

Going to Grandma's House

Get 2-sided counters. Use them to make 3 patterns to show the different paths that Red Riding Hood can take to get to Grandma's house. Ask a friend to tell about the pattern.

Name ______________________ Date ______________

IDENTIFYING GEOMETRIC PATTERNS

The Shape of Things to Come

Look at the patterns. Fill in the missing shapes. Write the pattern rule.

1. 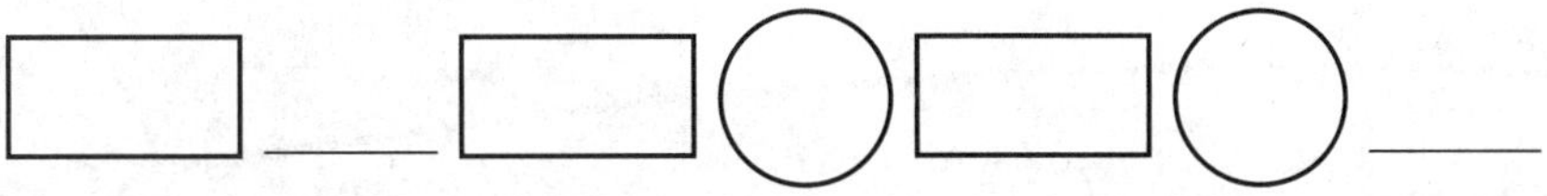

Rule: ______________________________________

2. 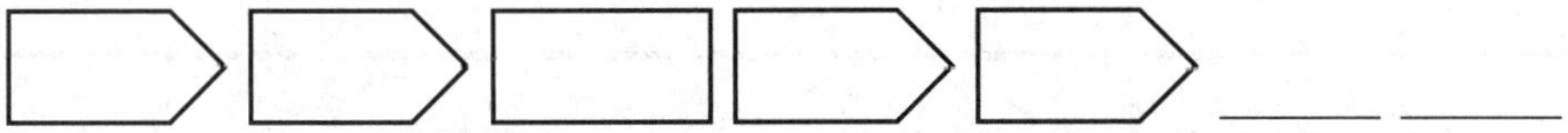

Rule: ______________________________________

3. 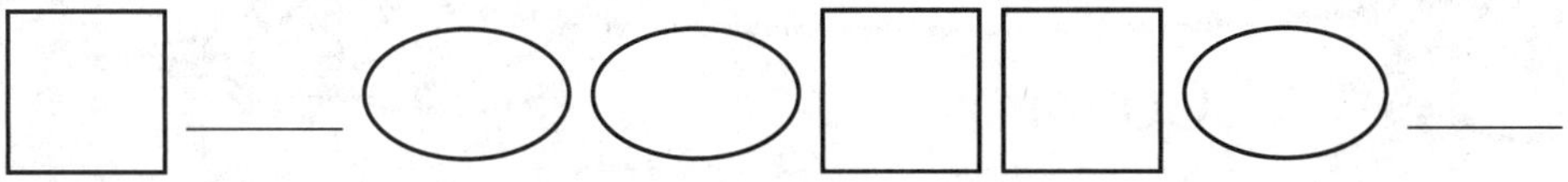

Rule: ______________________________________

4. 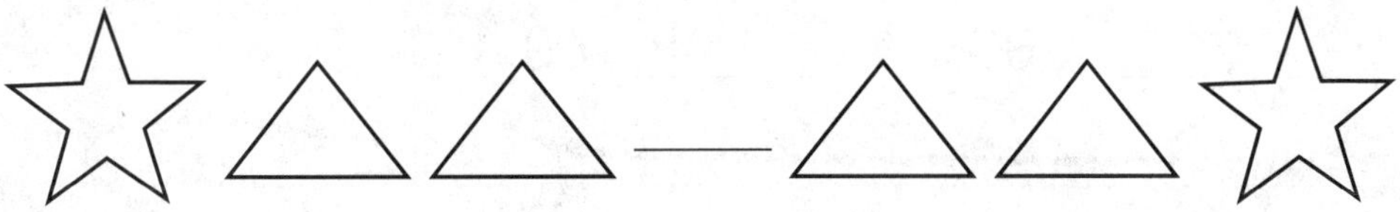

Rule: ______________________________________

5. 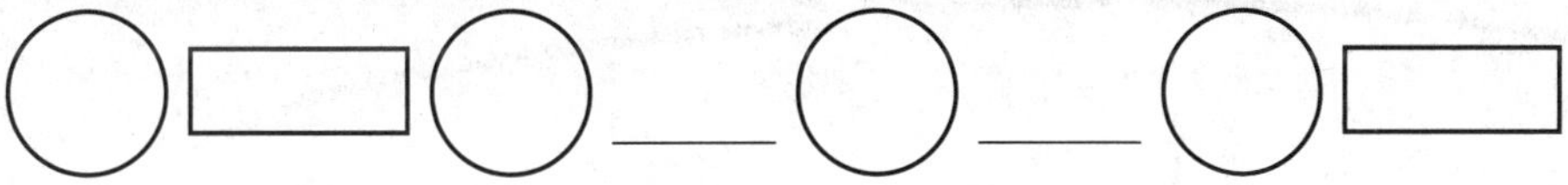

Rule: ______________________________________

Name ______________________ Date ______________

IDENTIFYING NUMBER PATTERNS

Your Number Is Up

➜ **Look at the patterns. Write the missing numbers. Write the rule.**

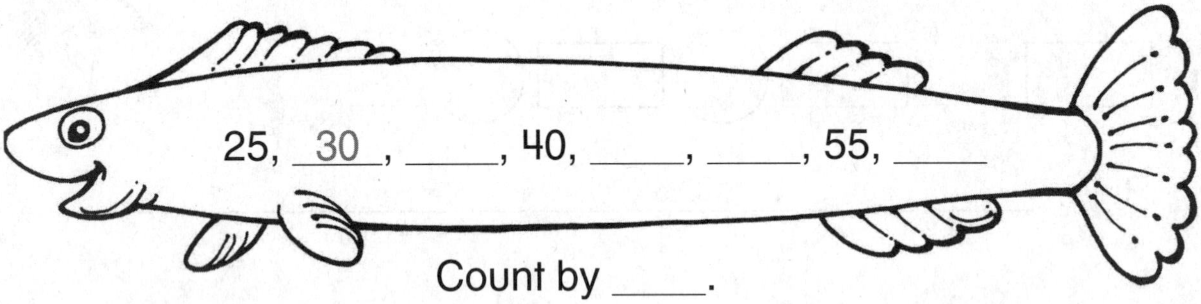

1. 25, __30__, ____, 40, ____, ____, 55, ____

Count by ____.

2. 22, ____, ____, 28, ____, ____, 34, ____, ____

Count by ____.

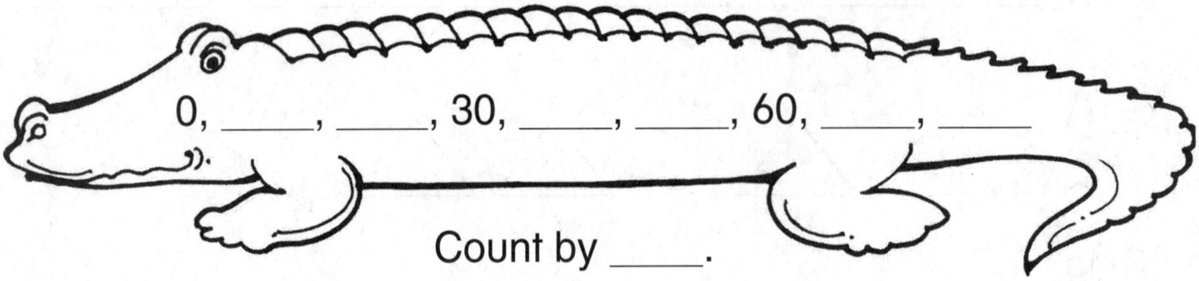

3. 0, ____, ____, 30, ____, ____, 60, ____, ____

Count by ____.

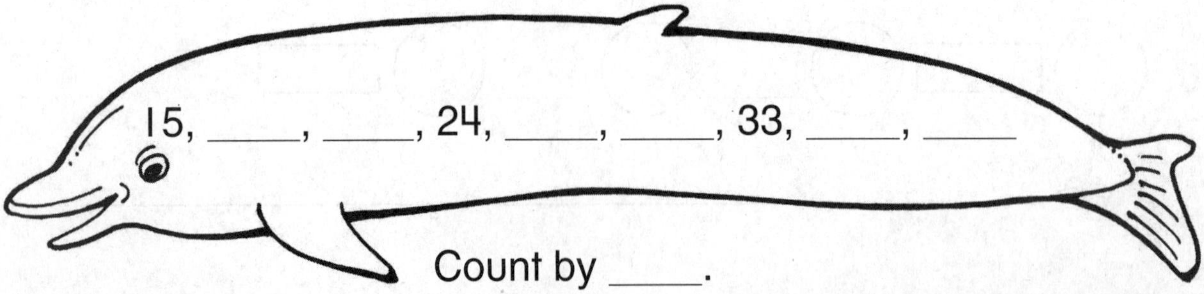

4. 15, ____, ____, 24, ____, ____, 33, ____, ____

Count by ____.

Name ______________________ Date ______________

FINDING NUMBER PATTERNS

Dot-to-Dot Farm

Count on by tens. Connect the dots to complete 5 things in the picture. Then color the picture.

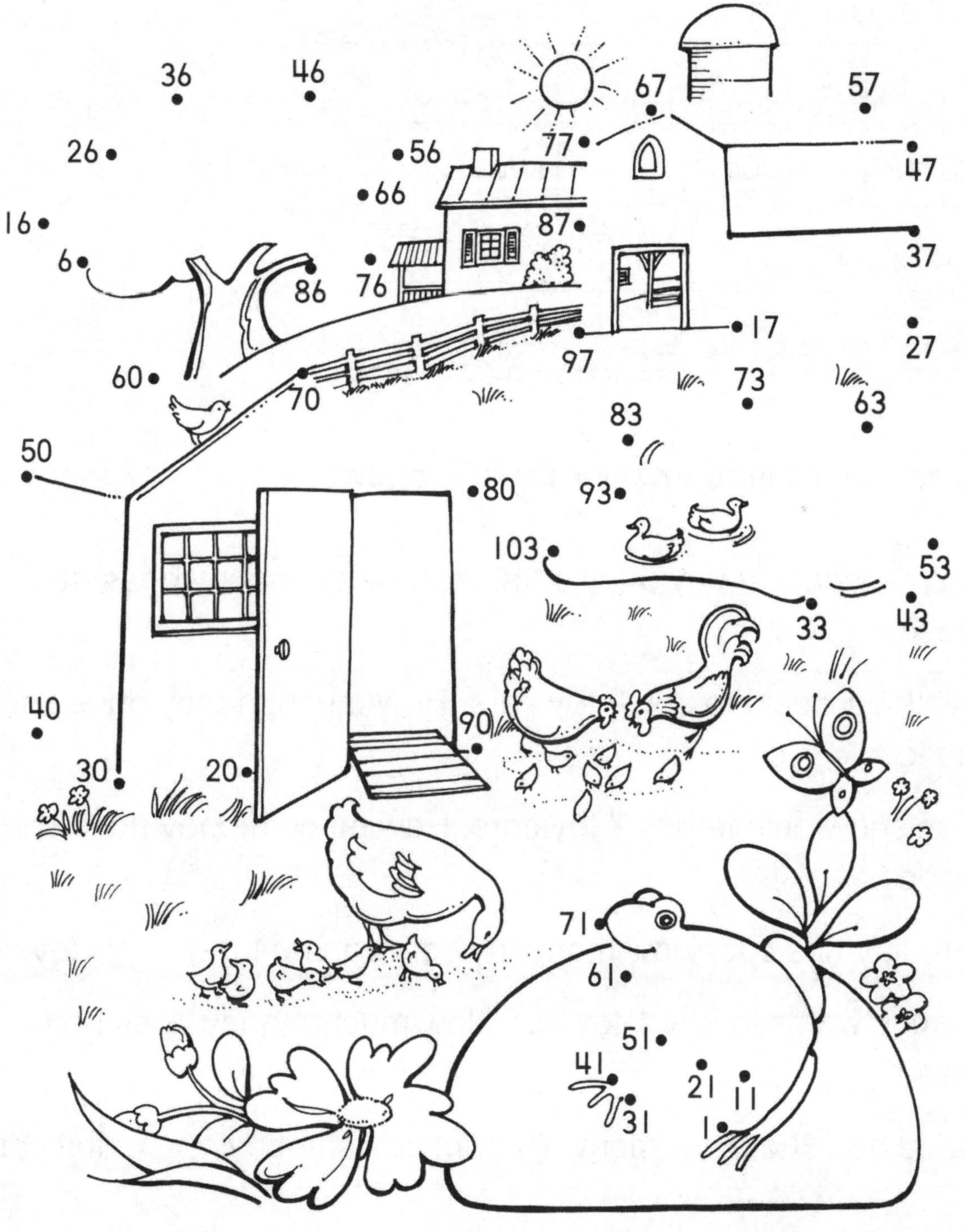

Name ______________________________ Date ______________

SOLVING WORD PROBLEMS

In the Toy Shop

Complete the table.

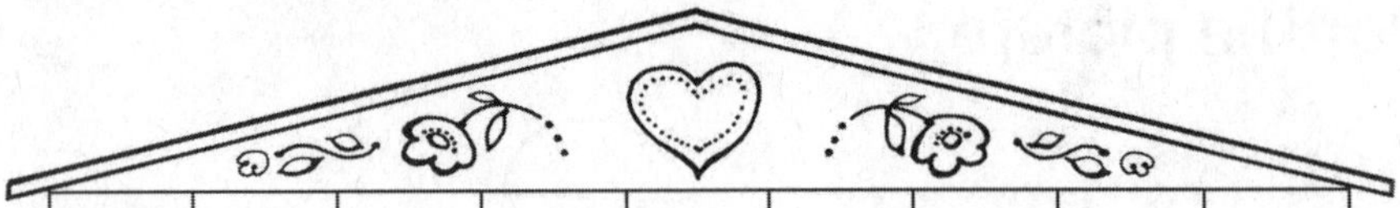

	1	2		4	5			8
	10¢		30¢			60¢		

Use the table to answer the questions.

1. Travis wants to buy 5 toy cars. How much money does he need? _____¢
2. Whitney wants to buy 4 toy cars. How much money does she need? _____¢
3. Tanisha wants to buy 7 toy cars. How much money does she need? _____¢
4. Bradley has 60¢. How many toy cars can he buy? _____ toy cars
5. Carlos wants to buy 1 toy car. How much money does he need? _____¢
6. Jade has 80¢. How many toy cars can she buy? _____ toy cars

Name ______________________ Date ______________

Finding Patterns on a 100 Chart

Look at the table. Tell about 3 number patterns that you see. Use another sheet of paper.

100 Chart

1	2	3	4	5	6	7	8	9	10
11	12	13	14	15	16	17	18	19	20
21	22	23	24	25	26	27	28	29	30
31	32	33	34	35	36	37	38	39	40
41	42	43	44	45	46	47	48	49	50
51	52	53	54	55	56	57	58	59	60
61	62	63	64	65	66	67	68	69	70
71	72	73	74	75	76	77	78	79	80
81	82	83	84	85	86	87	88	89	90
91	92	93	94	95	96	97	98	99	100

Lesson 7

Plane Figures

Objectives

- Count with understanding and recognize "how many" in sets of objects
- Sort, classify, and order objects by size, number, and other properties
- Recognize, name, build, draw, compare, and sort two- and three-dimensional shapes
- Describe attributes and parts of two- and three-dimensional shapes
- Investigate and predict the results of putting together and taking apart two- and three-dimensional shapes
- Describe, name, and interpret relative positions in space and apply ideas about relative position
- Recognize and apply slides, flips, and turns
- Recognize and create shapes that have symmetry
- Recognize and represent shapes from different perspectives
- Recognize geometric shapes and structures in the environment and specify their location
- Apply and adapt a variety of appropriate strategies to solve problems

Vocabulary

circle—a round plane figure that has no sides and no corners

congruent—figures that are the same shape and size

corner—the part of a figure where 2 sides meet

rectangle—a plane figure that has 4 sides and 4 corners. The opposite sides are the same length.

side—a straight line

square—a plane figure that has 4 sides, all of the same length, and 4 corners

triangle—a plane figure that has 3 sides and 3 corners

Materials

- scissors, crayons, pencils, pattern blocks (optional), bags (optional), paper clips (optional), rulers (optional)

Lesson Pages

Page 56 **(Manipulatives)**
Children cut out tangram pieces and use them to build figures.

Page 57 **(Practice)**
To begin to understand characteristics of figures, children color and count sides and corners.

Page 58 **(Practice)**
Children draw figures that are the same size and shape on geoboards.

Page 59 **(Extension)**
Children begin to explore flips, slides, and turns as they count the number of shapes that will fit inside plane figures.

Page 60 **(Word Problems)**
Children follow instructions and solve word problems.

Page 61 **(Enrichment)**
Activity Card 1: To develop visual thinking, children count plane figures, some of which are partly hidden.
Activity Card 2: Children draw a picture using squares, triangles, circles, and rectangles and identify the number of each in the picture.

Another Look

- Invite partners to take turns making patterns with pattern blocks. One child forms the pattern. The partner points to and names each shape, and then extends the pattern. (Visual, Kinesthetic, ELL)
- Place pattern blocks, one for each child, inside a bag. Invite each child to choose a shape without looking and name it before pulling it out. (Visual, Kinesthetic, ELL)

Extension

- Provide pattern blocks and challenge children to use the smaller figures to form larger, different figures. For example, two squares form a rectangle. Have children trace the blocks to show the combinations.
- Enlarge the tangram pieces on page 56 to fill the page. Invite children to measure the individual pieces with paper clips or rulers to find the perimeters.

At Home

- Send home copies of the tangram pieces on page 56. Challenge children to make different figures using all the pieces and trace the perimeters on paper. Ask them to share the figures with a family member and name the shapes they used.
- Tell children to go on a food hunt. Challenge them to find 5 foods that have shapes they know. Ask them to draw the food. If time permits during the following day, have them match pattern blocks to the drawings.
- Visit www.harcourtachieve.com/achievementzone for additional ideas and activity pages.

Answer Key

Page 56
Check children's figures.

Page 57
1. 4; 4
2. 0; 0
3. 3; 3
4. 4; 4
5. 4; 4
6. 3; 3

Page 58
Check that children draw figures that are the same size and shape.

Page 59
1. 15
2. 26
3. 22; 132
4. Answers will vary.

Page 60
1. Children circle the rectangular rug.
2. 2
3. Children circle the square.
4. Check children's answers

Page 61
Card 1
1. circles: 3
triangles: 5
rectangles: 1
squares: 4
2. Answers may vary slightly.
circles: 6
triangles: 4
rectangles or squares: 2
Card 2: Answers will vary.

Name ______________________ Date ______________

EXPLORING PLANE FIGURES

Picture Some Shapes

Cut out the tangram pieces. Use them to build each figure.

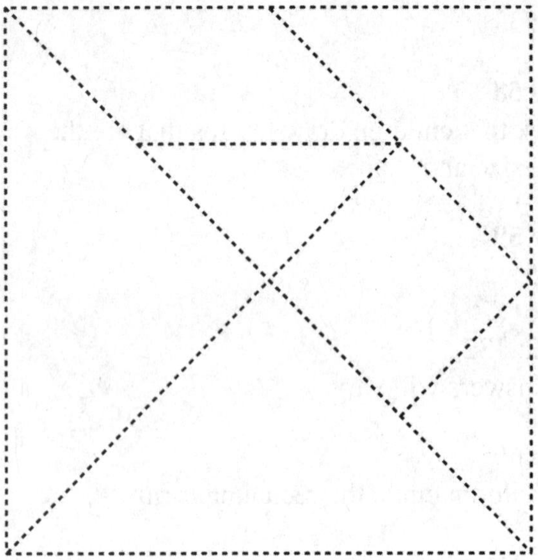

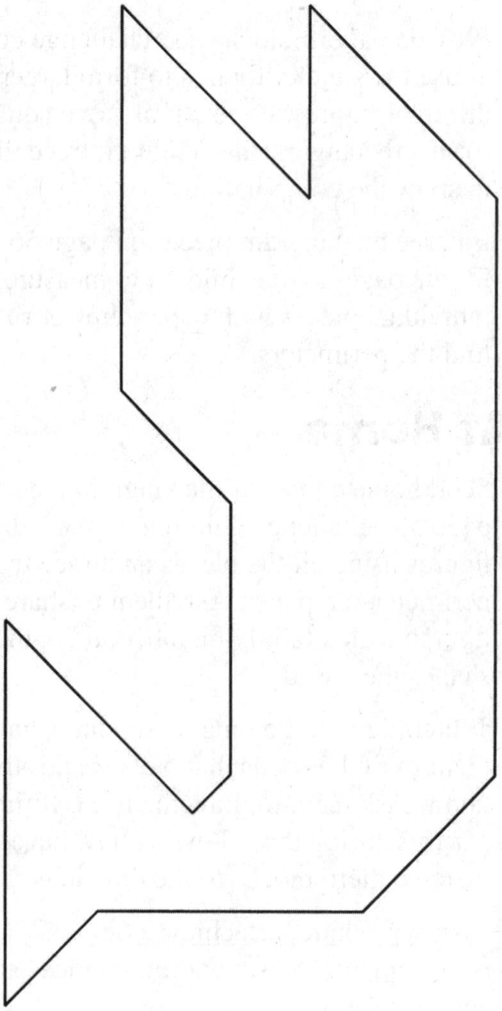

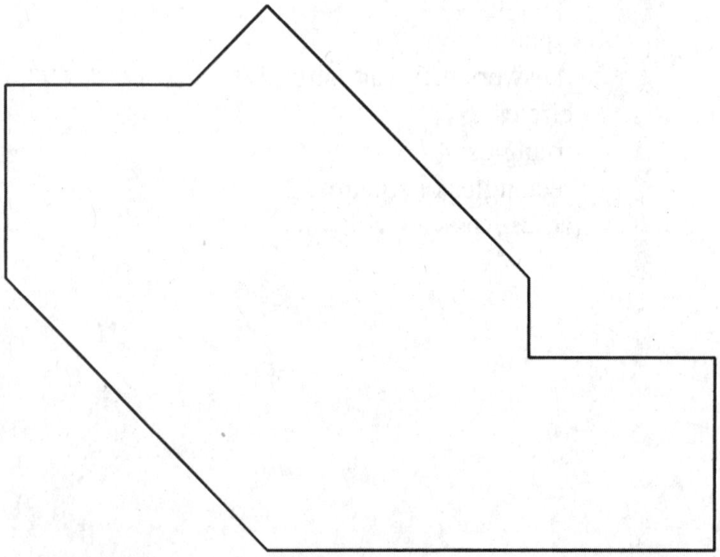

Name ______________________ Date ______________

IDENTIFYING SIDES AND CORNERS

Sides and Corners

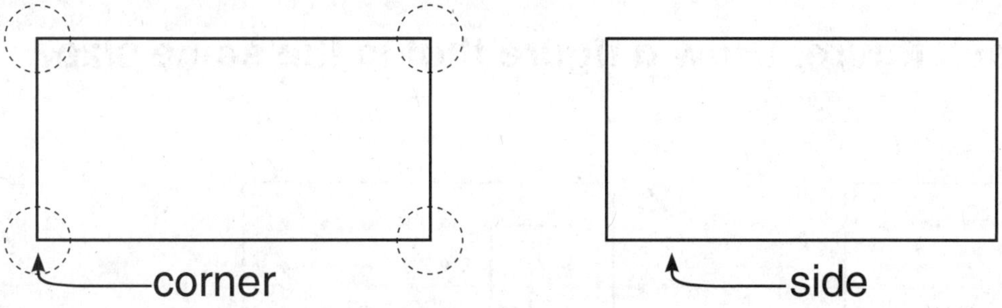

➔ **Draw a red circle on each corner. Trace each side blue. Then write how many sides and corners.**

1. 

__4__ sides
__4__ corners

2. 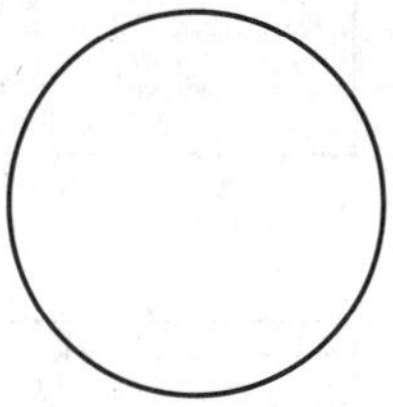

_____ sides
_____ corners

3. 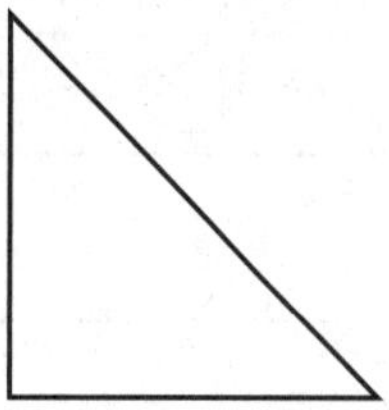

_____ sides
_____ corners

4. 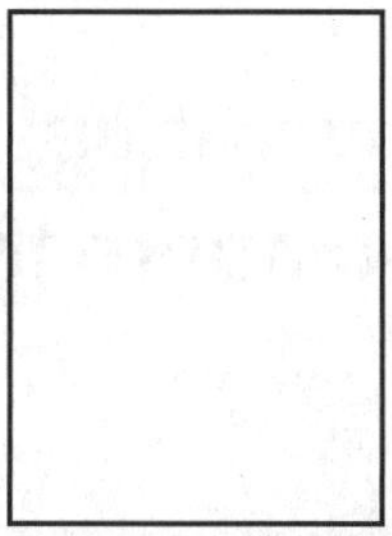

_____ sides
_____ corners

5. 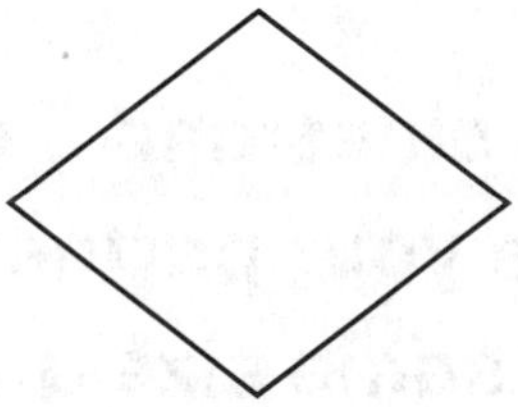

_____ sides
_____ corners

6. 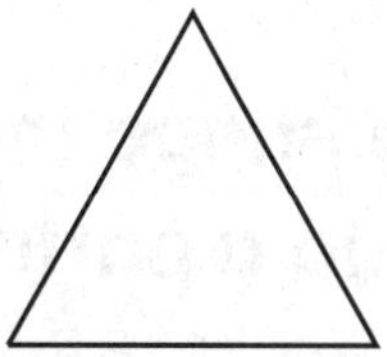

_____ sides
_____ corners

Name ______________________________ Date ______________

IDENTIFYING CONGRUENT FIGURES

These Corners Count

Look at each figure. Draw a figure that is the same size and shape.

1. 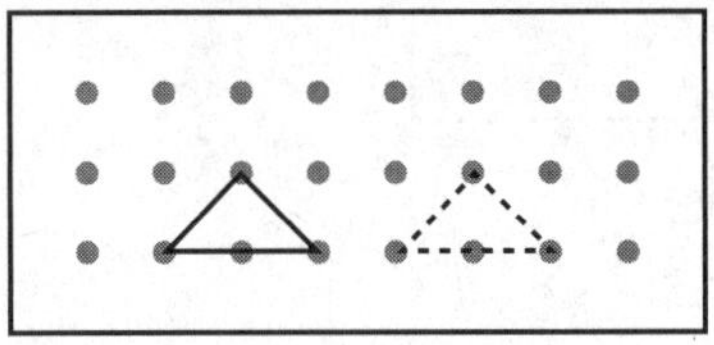

2. 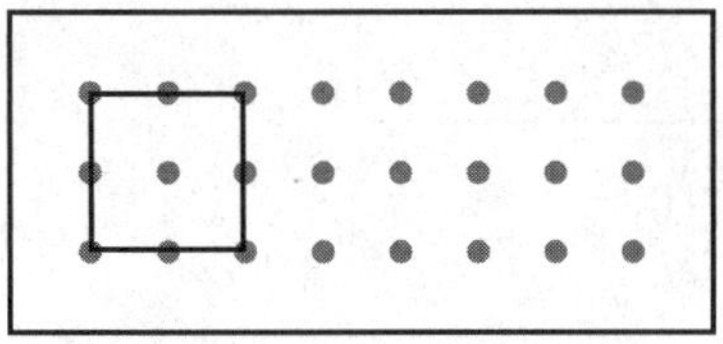

3. 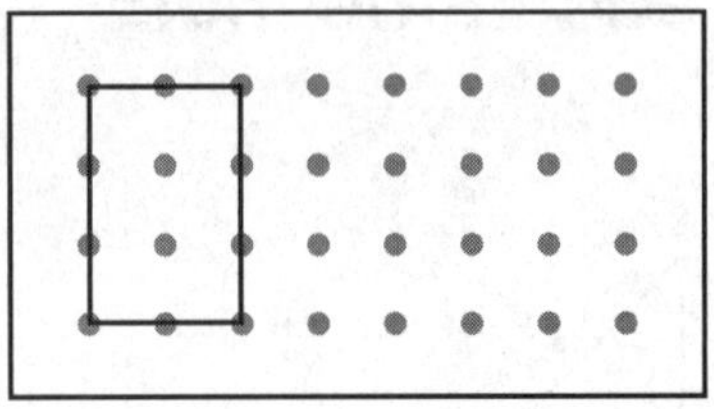

4. 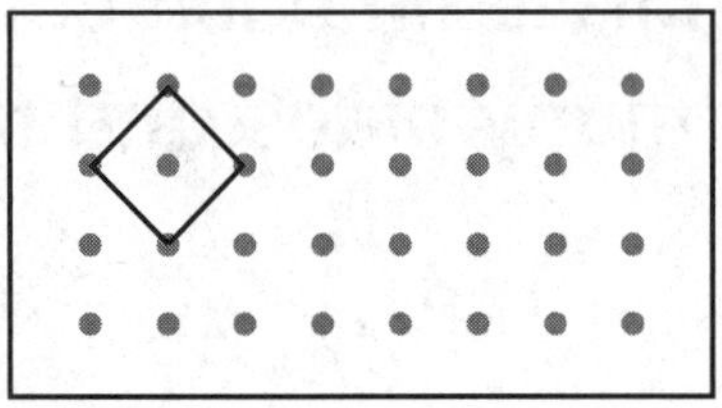

5. 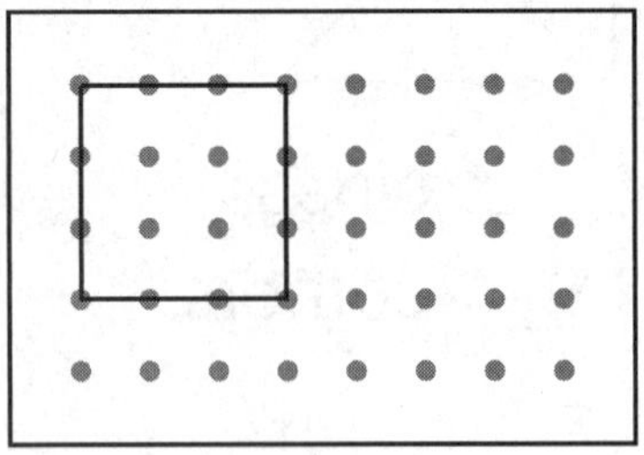

6. 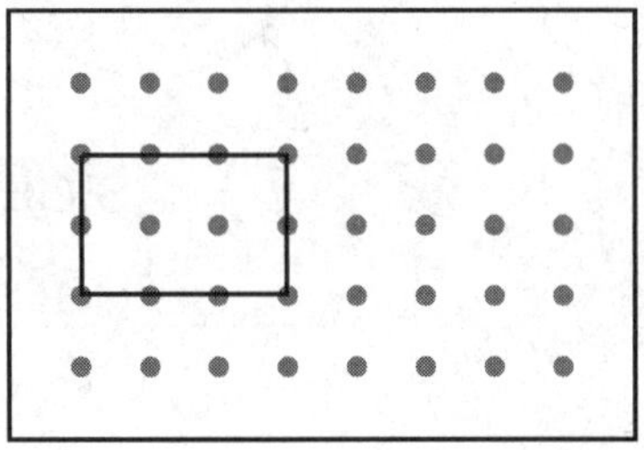

Draw a shape that has 3 sides and 3 corners. Cover it up. Describe it to a partner. Have your partner draw it. Compare the shapes to see if they are the same size and shape.

7. 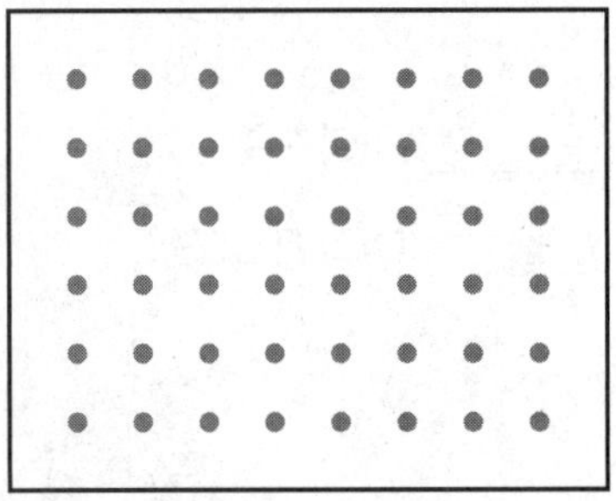

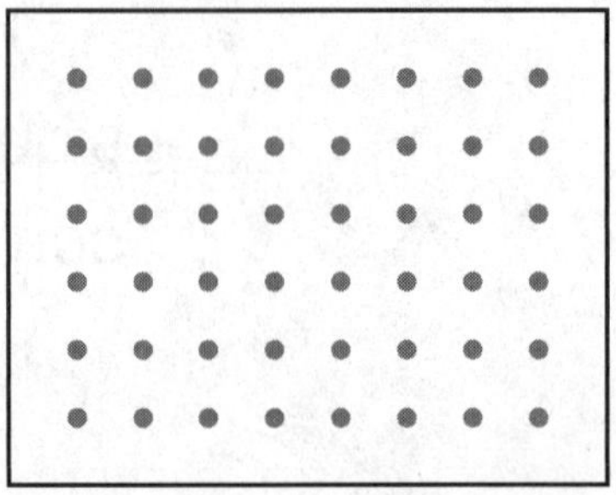

Name ______________________ Date ______________

EXPLORING FLIPS, SLIDES, AND TURNS

How Many Shapes?

Look at the shaded shape in each box. Count the total number of that shape that will fit inside the other shapes in each row. Draw lines and shade in each area to help you.

1.

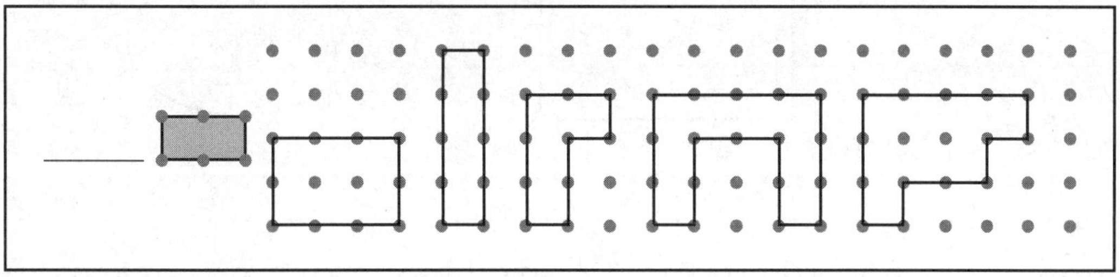

2.

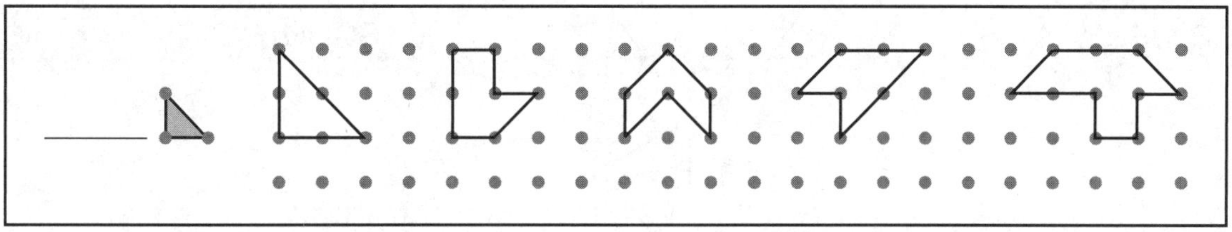

3.

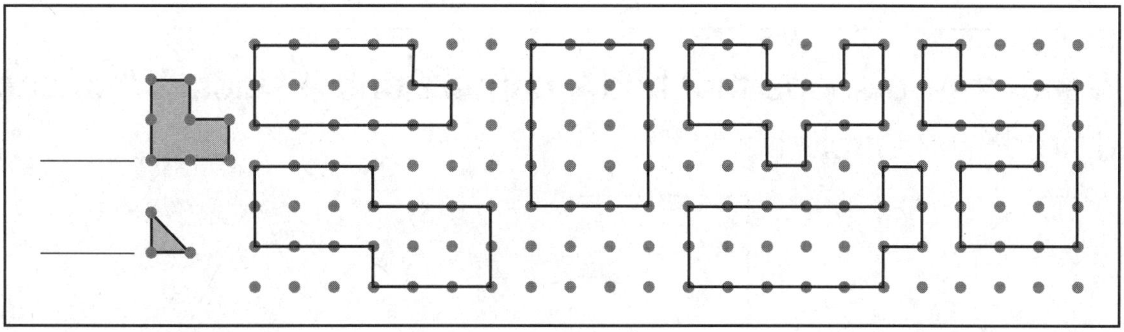

Make your own shapes.

4.

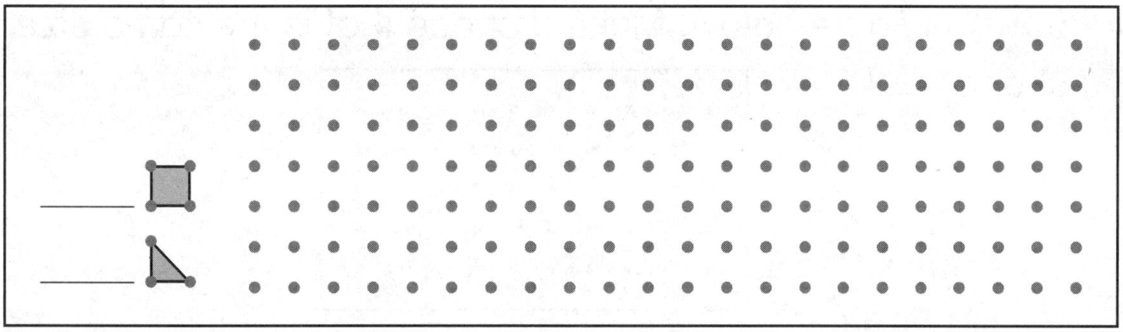

Name ________________________________ Date ________________

SOLVING WORD PROBLEMS

Problem Solving Takes Shape

Read each story. Solve.

1. Leo buys a rug that is shaped like a rectangle. Circle it.

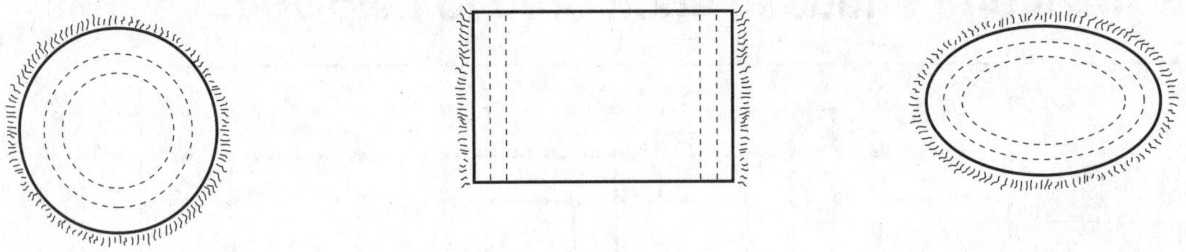

2. Anne uses shapes to make this figure. How many squares does she use? ____ squares

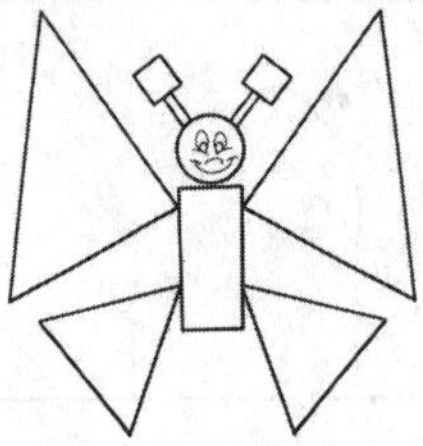

3. Alfredo drew a shape that had 4 corners and 4 sides. What shape did he draw? Circle it.

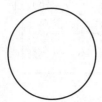

4. Tia drew the figure below. Make a shape that is the same size and shape.

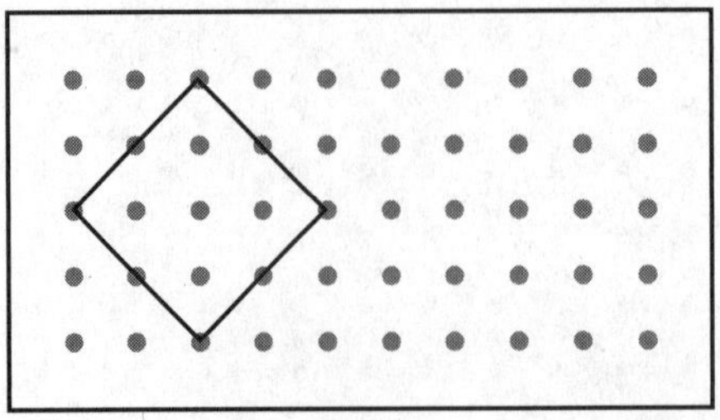

Name ______________________ Date ____________

Making Plane Figures

Look at the shape. Answer the questions.

1. How many do you see?

_____ circles _____ triangles

_____ rectangles _____ squares

2. How many are partly hidden?

_____ circles _____ triangles

_____ rectangles or squares

Name ______________________ Date ____________

Shaping a Picture

Draw a picture using squares, triangles, circles, and rectangles on another sheet of paper. The figures can be different sizes as in the picture below. Tell how many of each shape you use.

_____ triangles _____ squares

_____ circles _____ rectangles

Lesson 8

Solid Figures

Objectives

- Sort, classify, and order objects by size, number, and other properties
- Recognize, name, build, draw, compare, and sort two- and three-dimensional shapes
- Describe attributes and parts of two- and three-dimensional shapes
- Investigate and predict the results of putting together and taking apart two- and three-dimensional shapes
- Recognize and represent shapes from different perspectives
- Recognize geometric shapes and structures in the environment and specify their location
- Apply and adapt a variety of appropriate strategies to solve problems

Vocabulary

cone—a three-dimensional figure that has 1 flat face shaped like a circle

cube—a three-dimensional figure that has 6 flat faces that are square shaped; having a block shape

cylinder—a three-dimensional figure that has 2 flat faces that are circle shaped; having a can shape

face—the flat side of a figure

pyramid—a three-dimensional figure that has 4 or 5 flat faces; one face is a triangle, rectangle or square; the other faces are triangles

rectangular prism—a three-dimensional figure that has 6 flat faces; having a box shape

sphere—a three-dimensional figure that has no flat faces; having a ball shape

Materials

- large three-dimensional shape blocks, pencils, crayons, tape (optional), permanent marker (optional), modeling clay (optional), toothpicks (optional), writing paper (optional), connecting cubes (optional), drawing paper (optional)

Lesson Pages

Page 64 **(Manipulatives)**
Children match shape blocks to items they often see around them. Then they tell how many flat faces each figure has.

Page 65 **(Practice)**
Children color the 2 figures that are the same. Then they name the figure.

Page 66 **(Practice)**
To develop an understanding of which shapes stack, children mark out the shapes that are not stacked properly.

Page 67 **(Extension)**
Children match flattened two-dimensional figures to their three-dimensional appearance.

Page 68 **(Word Problems)**
Children solve word problems.

Page 69 **(Enrichment)**
Activity Card 1: Children identify things that have specific shapes.
Activity Card 2: Children compare and contrast a cube and a rectangular prism.

Another Look

- Invite children to use the blocks to make patterns. Have them point to and name the figures as well as extend the pattern. (Visual, Kinesthetic, Auditory, ELL)
- Get large blocks. Use tape labels to number the sides. Have children trace the sides and label them with corresponding numbers. (Kinesthetic, Visual, ELL)

Extension

- Give children modeling clay and toothpicks. Have them make animals, real or imaginary, using basic geometric figures. Have them identify the figures they used. Encourage them to name the animal and describe where it lives and what it eats.
- Use connecting cubes to build various shapes with regular and irregular volumes. Have children guess and then count the blocks in each.

At Home

- Have children fold a piece of drawing paper into 4 quadrants. Have them label each section with *cube*, *cone*, *sphere*, and *cylinder*. Ask children to cut out pictures of items that have those shapes from recycled magazines or newspapers and glue them in the correct box.
- Tell children to gather empty boxes and build with them. Have them draw a picture of the sculpture from the front and side.
- Visit www.harcourtachieve.com/achievementzone for additional ideas and activity pages.

Answer Key

Page 64
Check that children correctly match the block to the picture.

1. 1
2. 2
3. 6
4. 0
5. 5
6. 6

Page 65

1. Children color the first and third figures.; rectangular prism
2. Children color the first and third figures.; pyramid
3. Children color the first and third figures.; cylinder
4. Children color the first and third figures.; cube
5. Children color the first and third figures.; cone
6. Children color the second and third figures.; sphere

Page 66
Children cross out numbers 1, 3, 4, and 6.

Page 67

1. Children draw a line to the cube.
2. Children draw a line to the pyramid.
3. Children draw a line to the cylinder.
4. Children draw a line to the cone.

Page 68

1. Children color the third, flat box.
2. Children circle the cylinder.
3. Children circle the cube.
4. Children circle "circle."

Page 69
Card 1: Answers will vary.
Card 2: 6; 6

1. Possible answer: They both have 6 faces and 8 corners.
2. Possible answer: The faces of the cube are all the same size. There are 4 faces that are the same size on the prism.

Name ______________________________ Date ______________

IDENTIFYING SOLIDS

Block Sort

➜ Get a , 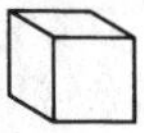, , , and 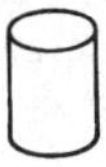. Match the blocks to the pictures. Then write how many faces.

1.

_____ flat faces

2.

_____ flat faces

3.

_____ flat faces

4.

_____ flat faces

5.

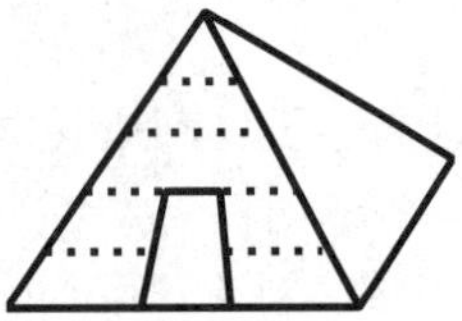

_____ flat faces

6.

_____ flat faces

Name ______________________ Date ______________

IDENTIFYING SOLIDS

Make a Match

Color the figures that are the same shape. Write the names of the figures.

cube sphere cone cylinder pyramid rectangular prism

1.

____

2.

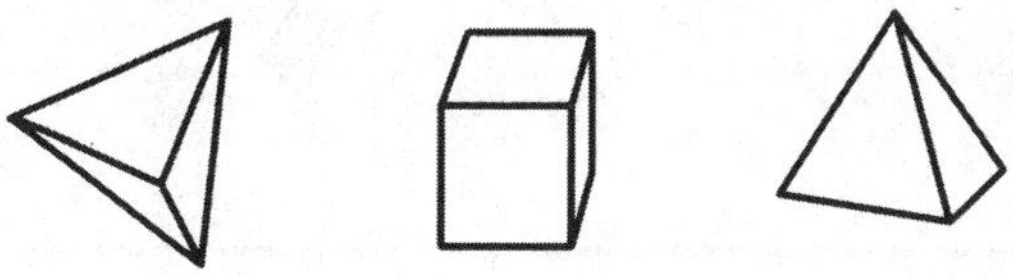

____

3.

____

4.

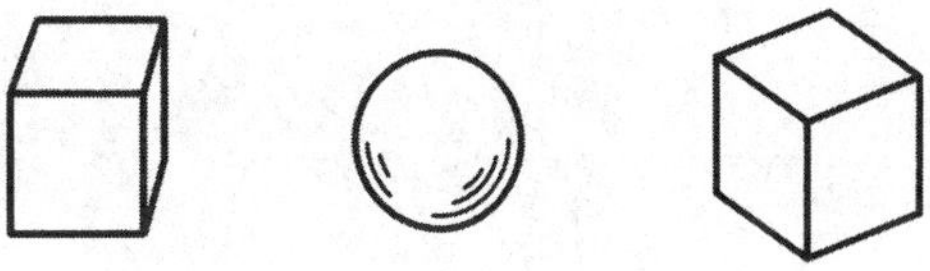

____

5.

____

6.

____

Name ______________________ Date ____________

UNDERSTANDING SOLIDS

Stack Them Up!

Cross out the stacks that could not be made.

1.

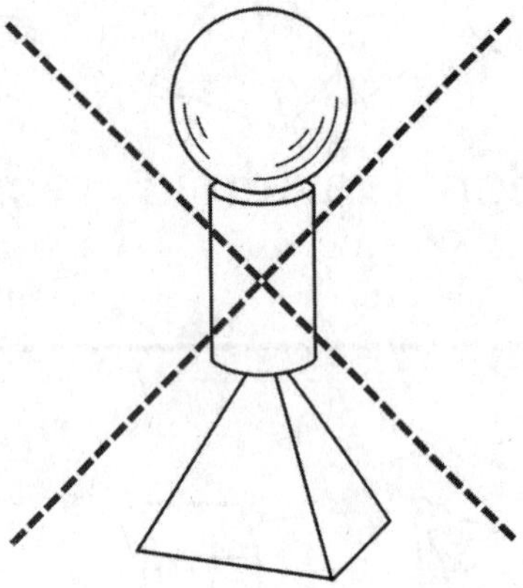

2.

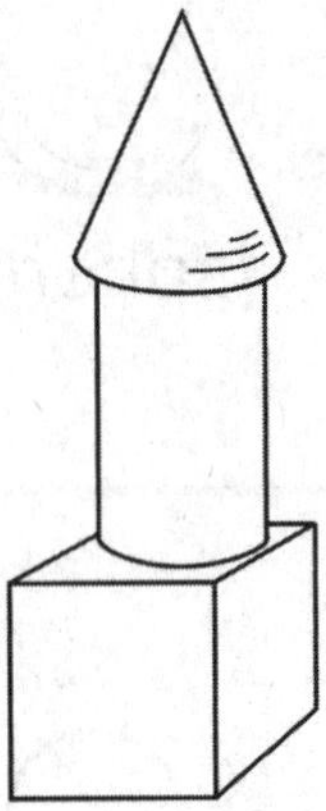

3.

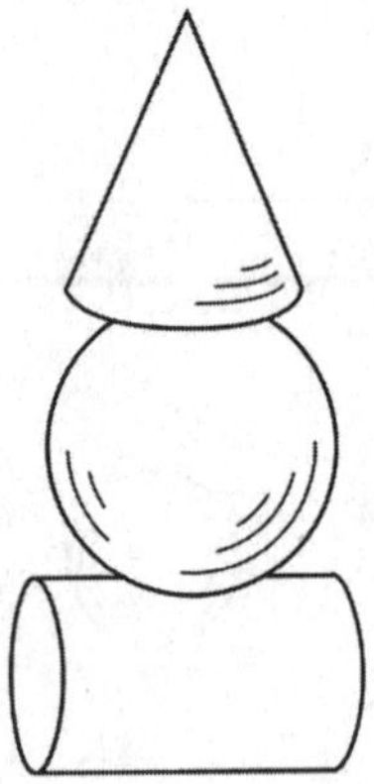

4.

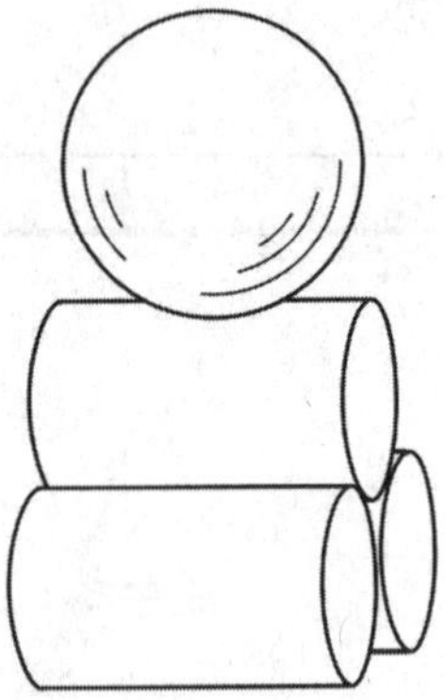

5.

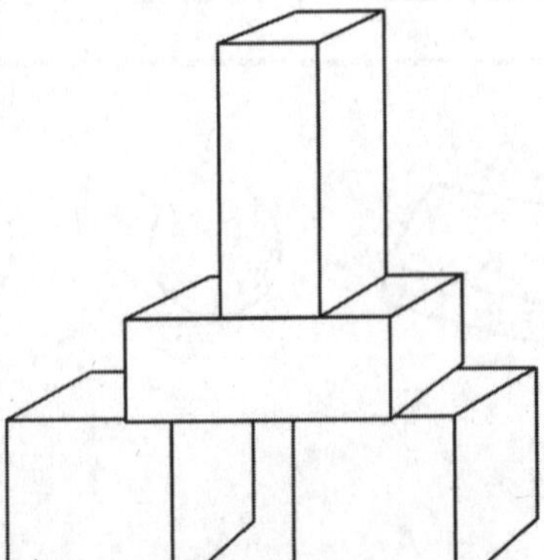

6.

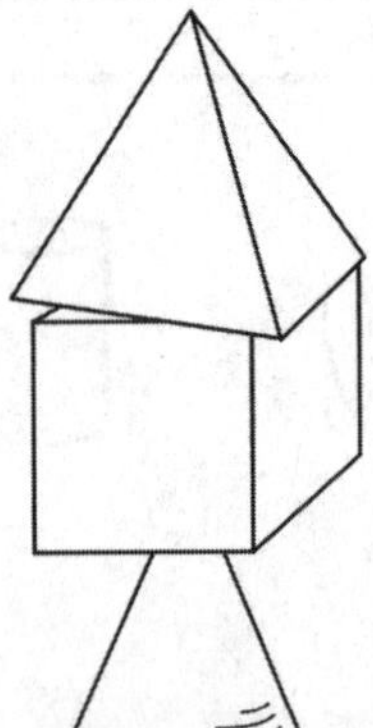

Name ______________________________ Date ______________

EXPLORING SOLIDS

Feeling Flat

Which solid shape could you make from each pattern? Draw lines to match.

1.

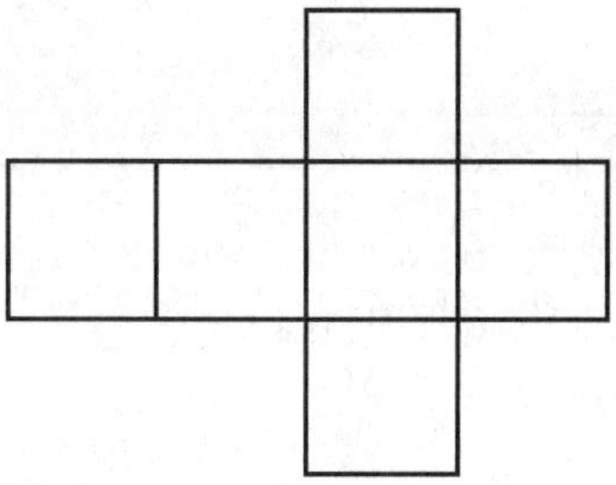

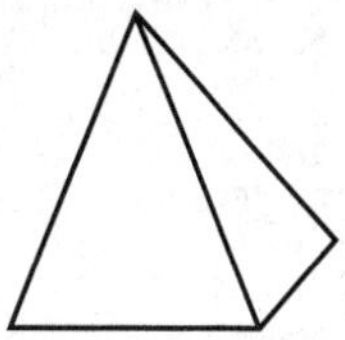

2.

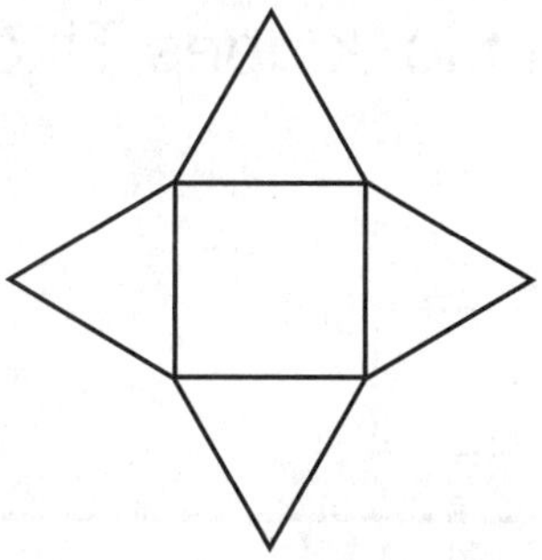

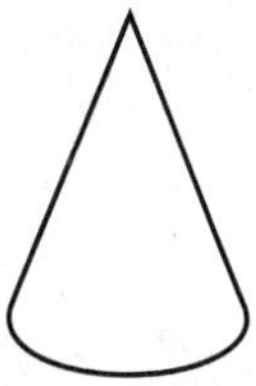

3.

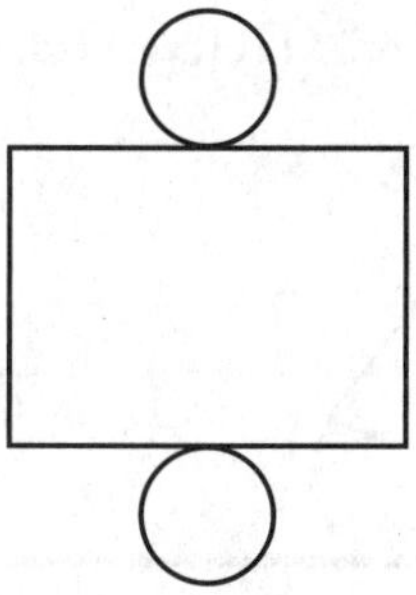

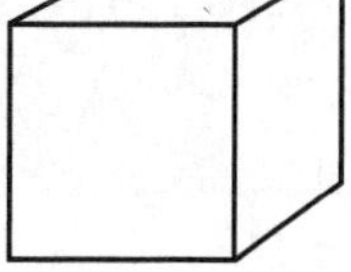

4.

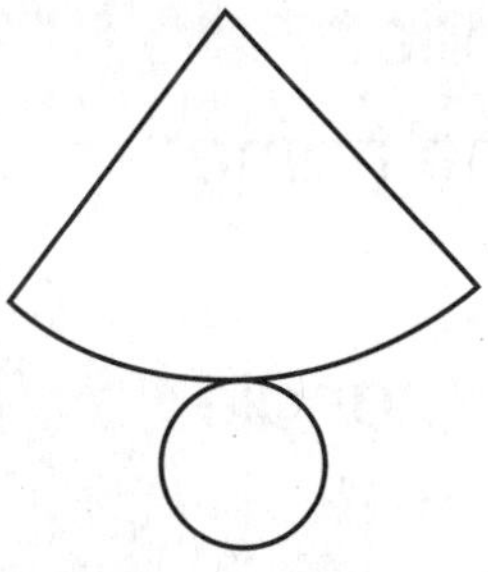

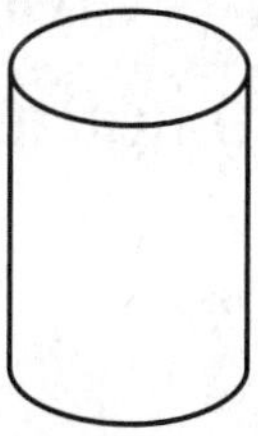

Name ______________________________ Date ________________

SOLVING WORD PROBLEMS

Blocks of Fun

Read each story. Solve.

1. Mark buys a book to give to a friend. In which box did he probably wrap the book? Color it.

2. Tina has a block. It has 2 flat faces. What block does Tina have? Circle it.

3. Sam uses these blocks to build. Which shape must he put on the bottom? Circle it.

4. Gloria traces around the widest part of a cone. What plane figure does she draw? Circle the name.

rectangle   circle   triangle

Name ______________________ Date ______________

Shaping Up

➜ **Look at each figure. Write 4 things that have each shape.**

1. 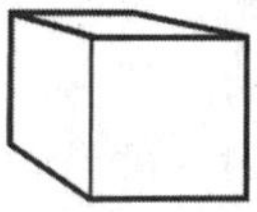

2. 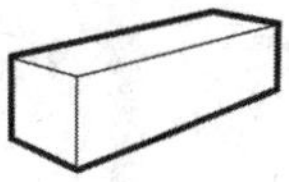

3. 

______________	______________	______________
______________	______________	______________
______________	______________	______________
______________	______________	______________

Name ______________________ Date ______________

Looking at Shapes

➜ **Look at each shape. Write how many faces. Then answer the questions.**

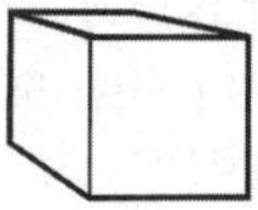 __________ faces

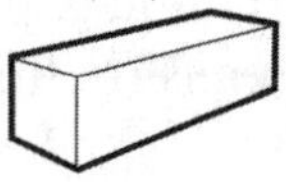 __________ faces

1. How are the shapes alike? ______________________________

____

2. How are the shapes different? ___________________________

____

Lesson 9

Symmetry

Objectives

- Recognize, name, build, draw, compare, and sort two- and three-dimensional shapes
- Describe attributes and parts of two- and three-dimensional shapes
- Investigate and predict the results of putting together and taking apart two- and three-dimensional shapes
- Recognize and create shapes that have symmetry
- Recognize and represent shapes from different perspectives
- Recognize geometric shapes and structures in the environment and specify their location
- Apply and adapt a variety of appropriate strategies to solve problems

Vocabulary

line of symmetry—an imaginary line that divides a figure into two parts that have exactly the same size and shape

symmetry—having two parts that match exactly

Materials

- scissors, pencils, crayons, construction paper shape cutouts (optional), dried beans (optional), glue (optional)

Lesson Pages

Page 72 **(Manipulatives)**
Children cut out 4 shapes and fold them along the dotted lines. Then they fold the shapes along another line of symmetry.

Page 73 **(Practice)**
Children draw lines to show symmetry.

Page 74 **(Practice)**
Children draw lines to show the different ways that a figure can show symmetry. Then they write how many lines of symmetry there are.

Page 75 **(Extension)**
Children find all the items in a park that have symmetry.

Page 76 **(Word Problems)**
Children solve word problems about symmetry.

Page 77 **(Enrichment)**
Activity Card 1: Children write the capital letters of the alphabet that have symmetry. Then they circle the ones that have two lines of symmetry.

Activity Card 2: Children identify the symmetry in words and then find 5 more words that have either a vertical or horizontal symmetry.

Another Look

- Cut out large, simple shapes from construction paper. Cut them in half. Have children match the shapes to see the lines of symmetry. (Visual, Kinesthetic, ELL)
- Cut out shapes from construction paper. Fold some equally and some unequally. Have children sort the shapes. (Visual, Kinesthetic, ELL)

Extension

- Invite children to glue dried beans to paper to make symmetrical designs.
- Invite children to fold a square of paper into fourths and cut out small shapes to make snowflakes. Encourage children to unfold their paper and describe the symmetry.

At Home

- Have children cut out pictures that show symmetry from recycled magazines or newspapers. Have them glue the pictures to paper and draw each line of symmetry.
- Tell children to find ways to cut food so the parts show symmetry. They can cut sandwiches, apples, and fruit bars.
- Visit www.harcourtachieve.com/achievementzone for additional ideas and activity pages.

Answer Key

Page 72
Children fold each shape along a second line of symmetry.

Page 73
Children draw lines of symmetry for the pictures.

Page 74
Children draw all the lines of symmetry for each picture.

1. 1
2. 1
3. 4
4. 2
5. 1
6. 3
7. 6
8. 1
9. 2
10. 1
11. 2
12. 2

Page 75
Answers may vary. Possible lines of symmetry: on the sun, evergreen tree, parallel bars, basketball goal, basketball, basketball court, swing set, football, and seesaw.

Page 76

1. Children circle the diamond.
2. Children draw a horizontal or vertical line of symmetry.
3. 4
4. no

Page 77
Card 1: Answers may vary.
One line of symmetry: A, B, C, D, E, H, I, K, M, O, T, U, V, W, X, Y
Two lines of symmetry: H, I, O, X
Card 2: *HAM* and *MOW* have vertical symmetry. *CODE* and *BOX* have horizontal symmetry. Words will vary.

Name ______________________ Date ______________

UNDERSTANDING SYMMETRY

Find and Fold

Cut out the shapes. Fold them on the line. See how the two sides match. Now find another line of symmetry. Fold the shapes on the new line.

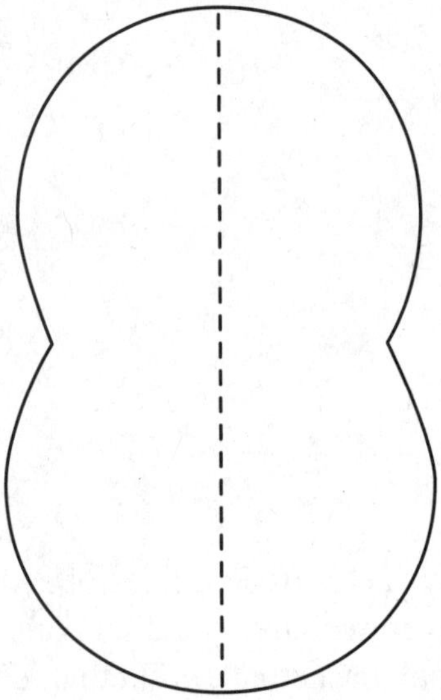

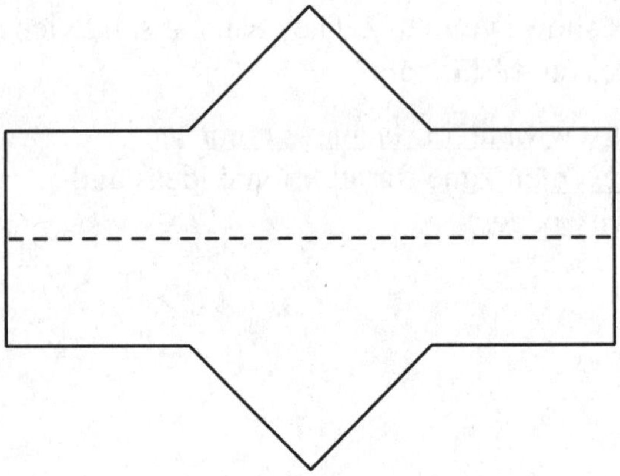

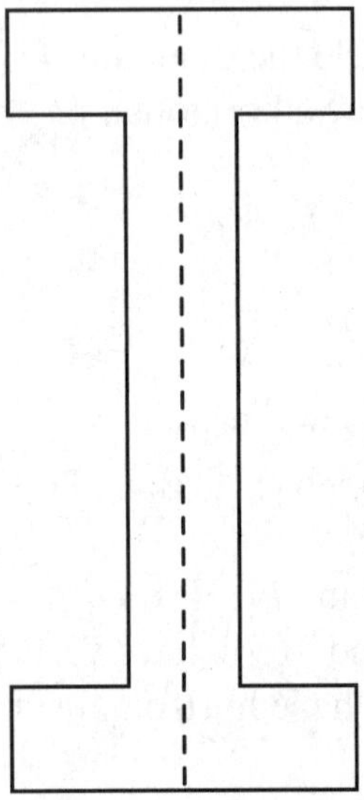

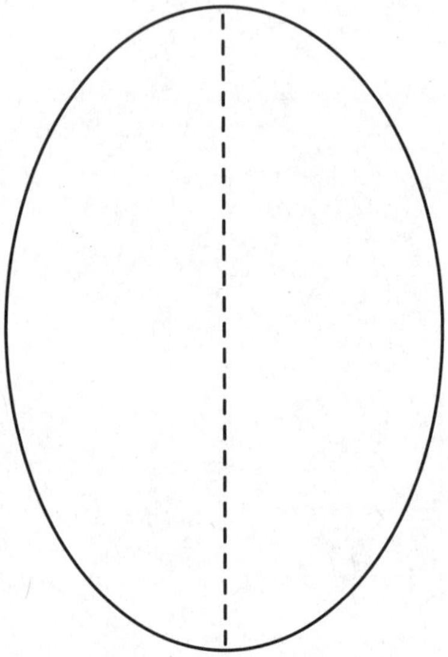

Name ______________________________ Date ______________

IDENTIFYING SYMMETRY

The Dividing Line

Draw one line of symmetry for each shape.

1.

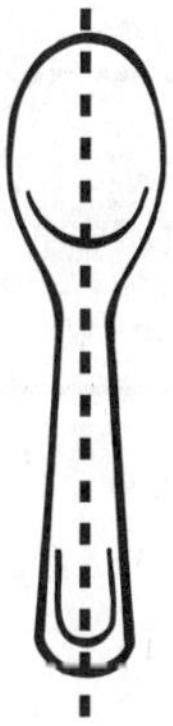

2.

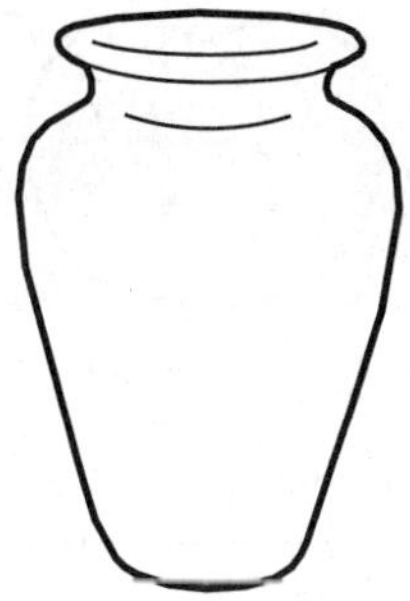

3.

4.

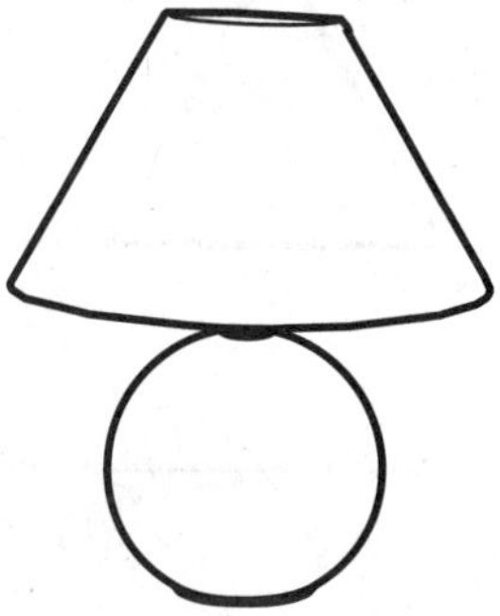

5.

6.

Draw two lines of symmetry for each shape.

7.

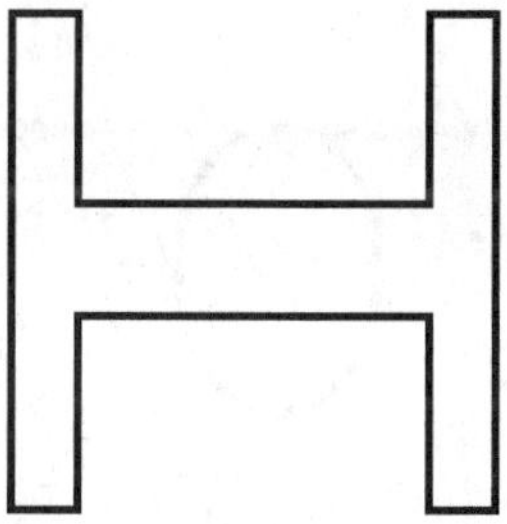

8.

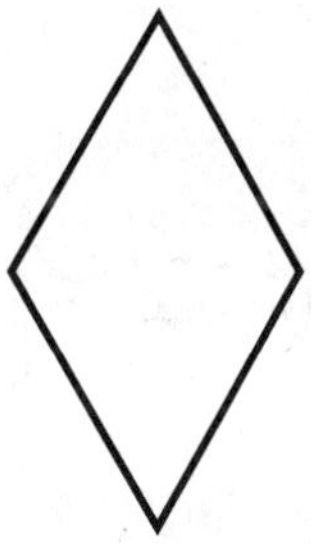

9.

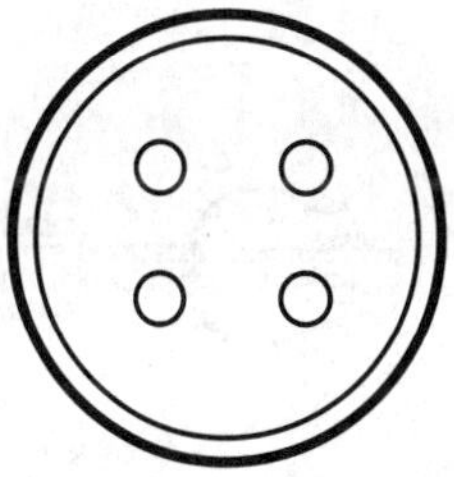

Name ______________________ Date ______________

PRACTICING SYMMETRY

Drawing the Line

Draw lines of symmetry. Write how many lines you drew.

1.

______

2.

______

3.

______

4.

______

5.

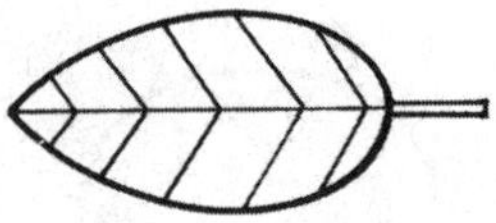

______

6.

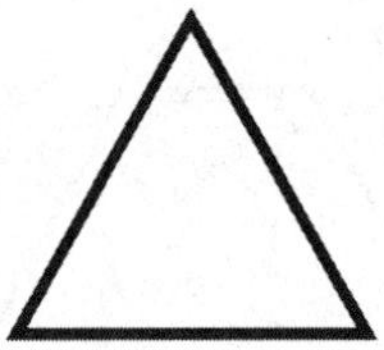

______

7.

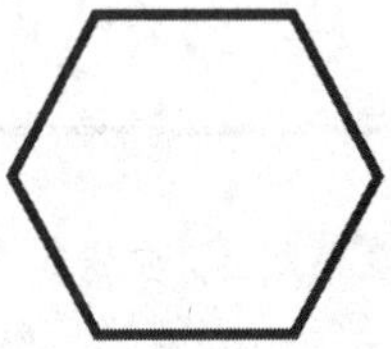

______

8.

______

9.

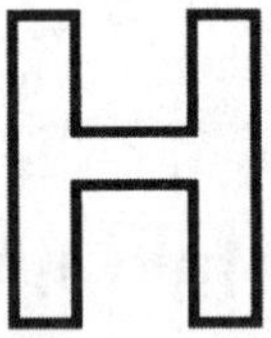

______

10.

______

11.

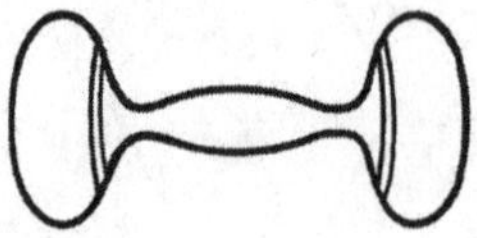

______

12.

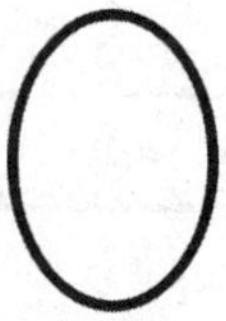

______

Name ______________________ Date ______________

FINDING SYMMETRY

Park Play

Find the things in the picture that have symmetry. Draw the line of symmetry. Then color the picture.

Name ______________________ Date ______________

SOLVING WORD PROBLEMS

Cut Ups

Read each story. Solve.

1. Sara cuts out this shape. What does it look like when she opens it? Circle it.

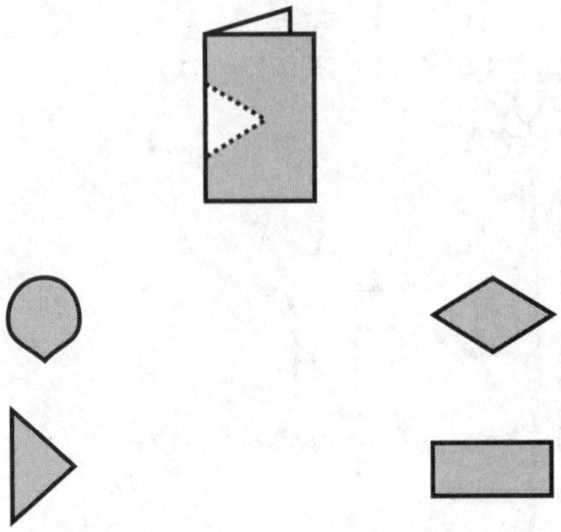

2. Amy cuts out this shape. She wants to make a card. Where will she fold it? Draw a line of symmetry.

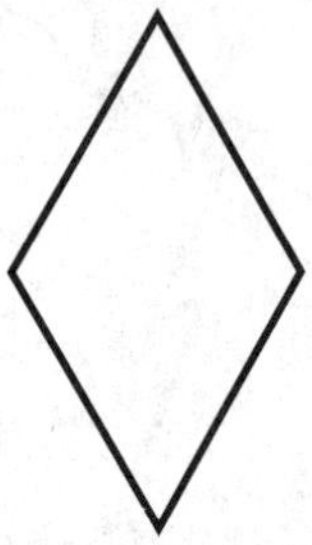

3. Ben cuts out this shape. How many lines of symmetry can he make?

4. Rolando cuts out this shape. Does it have a line of symmetry? Circle the answer.

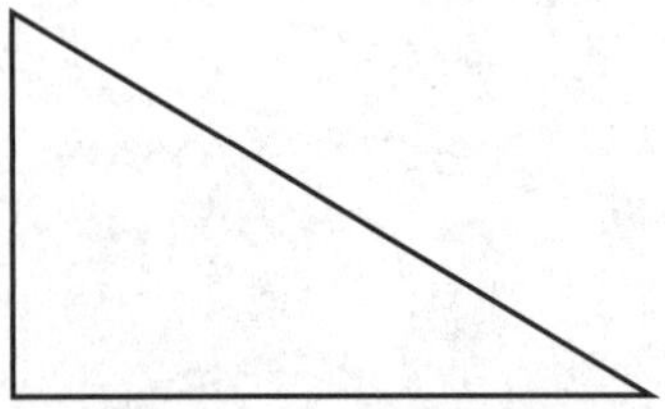

yes no

Name ______________________ Date ____________

Finding Letter Symmetry

➜ Think about the capital letters in the alphabet. Which letters are symmetrical? Write the letters below.

➜ Circle the letters that have two lines of symmetry.

Name ______________________ Date ____________

Making Word Symmetry

➜ Look at the words below. Draw a line of symmetry in each word. Then think of more words that have symmetry. Write at least 4 words that go down or across.

H	M	CODE	BOX
A	O		
M	W		

____

____

____

____

Lesson 10

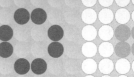

Fractions

Objectives

- Understand and represent commonly used fractions, such as $\frac{1}{4}$, $\frac{1}{3}$, and $\frac{1}{2}$
- Recognize, name, build, draw, compare, and sort two- and three-dimensional shapes
- Investigate and predict the results of putting together and taking apart two- and three-dimensional shapes
- Recognize and represent shapes from different perspectives
- Relate ideas in geometry to ideas in number and measurement
- Apply and adapt a variety of appropriate strategies to solve problems

Vocabulary

fraction—a way to describe equal parts of a whole or a group

Materials

- scissors, pencils, crayons, index cards (optional), connecting cubes (optional), plastic cups (optional), handmade spinner (optional), markers (optional), 2 colors of star stickers (optional), recycled wallpaper pattern books (optional)

Lesson Pages

Page 80 **(Manipulatives)**
Children cut out halves, thirds, and fourths of circles and put them together to form fraction circles.

Page 81 **(Practice)**
Children write fractions to show the number of shaded parts.

Page 82 **(Practice)**
Children color figures to show the given fraction.

Page 83 **(Extension)**
Children look at pictures to solve word problems.

Page 84 **(Word Problems)**
Children solve word problems about fractions.

Page 85 **(Enrichment)**
Activity Card 1: Children find the fractional parts of a divided triangle.
Activity Card 2: Children draw lines to match fractional parts of time to the movement of a clock.

Another Look

- Make cards showing the fractions $\frac{1}{2}$, $\frac{1}{3}$, and $\frac{1}{4}$. Put two colors of connecting cubes into plastic cups showing the fractional amounts, but do not connect the cubes. Children put the cubes together and match a fraction card with the value. (Visual, Kinesthetic, ELL)
- Make a spinner showing the fractions $\frac{1}{2}$, $\frac{1}{3}$, and $\frac{1}{4}$. Have groups of children use their fraction circles from page 80. Children take turns spinning and forming the circles. The first player to put together all three circles wins. (Visual, Kinesthetic, ELL)

Extension

- Make cards showing all fraction combinations of halves, thirds, and fourths. (Fourths would be $\frac{1}{4}$, $\frac{2}{4}$, $\frac{3}{4}$, and $\frac{4}{4}$.) Use star stickers to make corresponding picture cards. Invite children to play Concentration to match the fraction to the picture card.
- Invite children to make quilt blocks. Ask each child to choose from one to four different wallpaper patterns. Have them cut the wallpaper into two-inch squares. Have them glue the squares on paper to form a quilt pattern. Tell them to write the fractions to show how many of each pattern they used.

At Home

- Ask children to choose a picture from a magazine or newspaper. Tell them to cut it into 2, 3, or 4 equal pieces to make a puzzle. Have children tell a family member if the puzzle is in halves, thirds, or fourths.
- Tell children to look for ways to divide food items into halves, thirds, and fourths. For snacks, they can cut apples, oranges, and even peanut butter sandwiches.
- Visit www.harcourtachieve.com/achievementzone for additional ideas and activity pages.

Answer Key

Page 80
Children cut out and put together shapes to make fraction circles.

Page 81

1. 2	**2.** 2
3. 1	**4.** 3
5. 4	**6.** 5
7. $\frac{3}{4}$	**8.** $\frac{2}{10}$
9. $\frac{2}{3}$	**10.** $\frac{3}{5}$
11. $\frac{6}{8}$	**12.** $\frac{4}{10}$

Page 82

1. Children color 1 part of each figure.
2. Children color 1 part of each figure.
3. Children color 1 part of each figure.
4. Children color to show these parts: 1 part, 2 parts, 3 parts, 4 parts.

Page 83

1. $\frac{3}{5}$, $\frac{2}{5}$
2. $\frac{2}{6}$, $\frac{4}{6}$
3. $\frac{6}{7}$, $\frac{1}{7}$
4. $\frac{6}{8}$, $\frac{3}{8}$

Page 84

1. Children draw a shape and divide it into 3 equal parts.
2. $\frac{1}{4}$
3. $\frac{1}{3}$
4. $\frac{1}{4}$

Page 85
Card 1: Check children's triangles.
Card 2: Children draw lines from the clock to these times:

1. $\frac{1}{2}$ past the hour
2. $\frac{1}{4}$ past the hour
3. $\frac{3}{4}$ past the hour

Name ______________________ Date ______________

UNDERSTANDING FRACTIONS

Rounding Up Fractions

Cut out the shapes. Put the shapes together to make circles. How many equal parts in each circle?

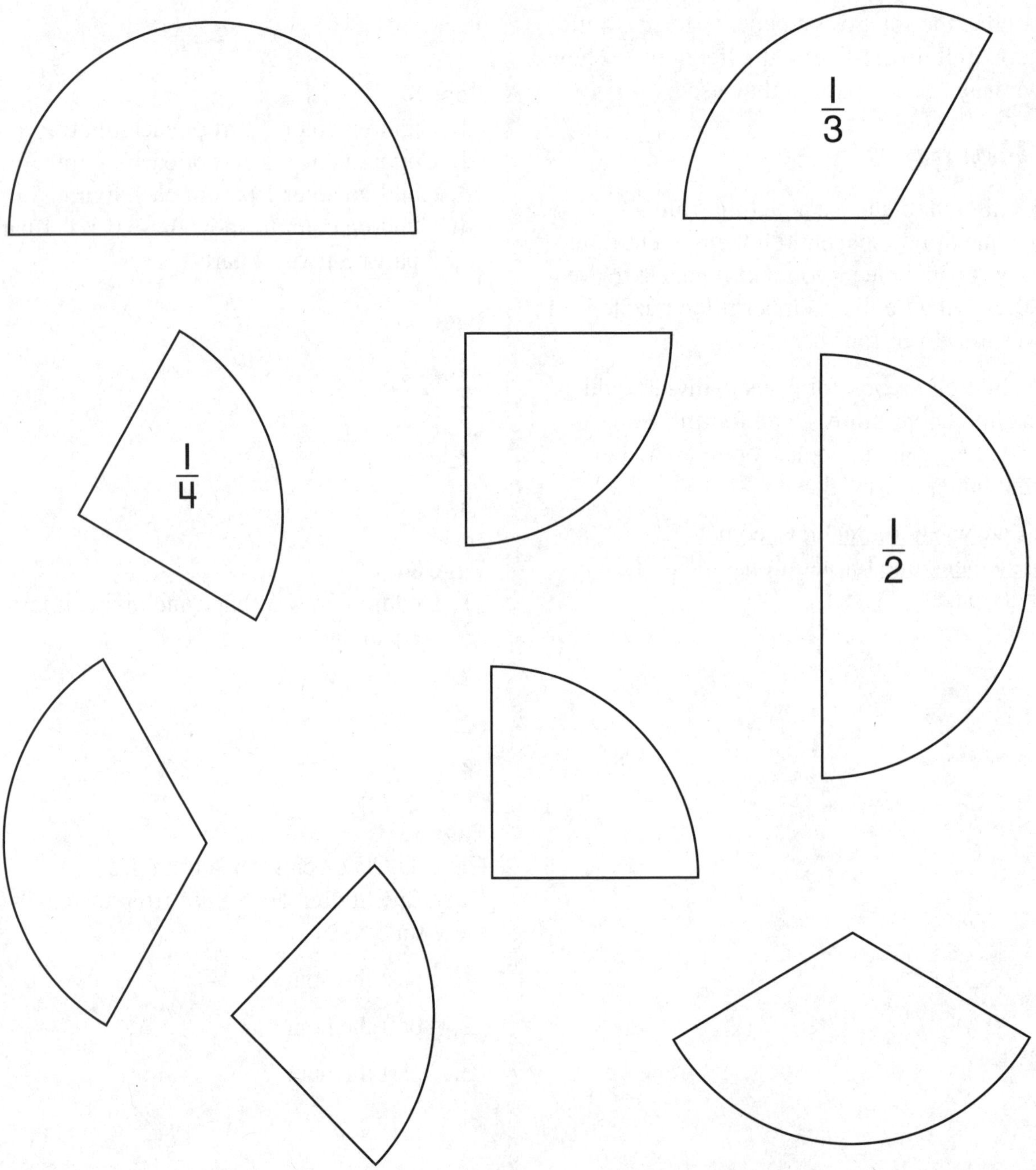

Name ________________________ Date ______________

WRITING FRACTIONS

Shady Fractions

What part is shaded? Complete the fraction.

1. 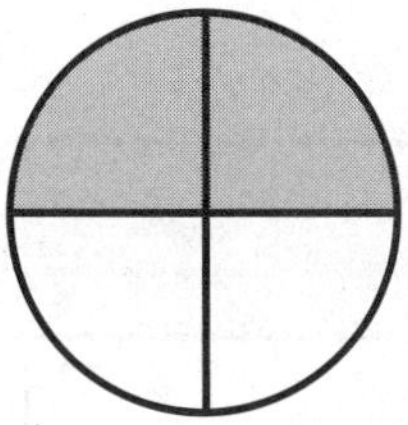

$\frac{2}{4}$

2. 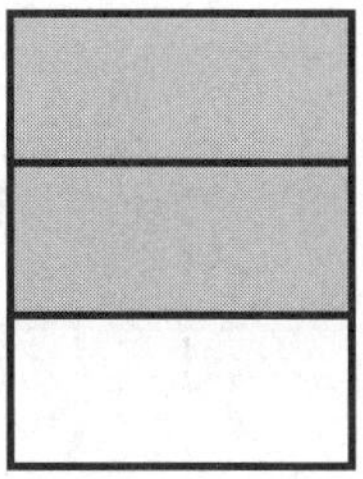

$\frac{\bigcirc}{3}$

3. 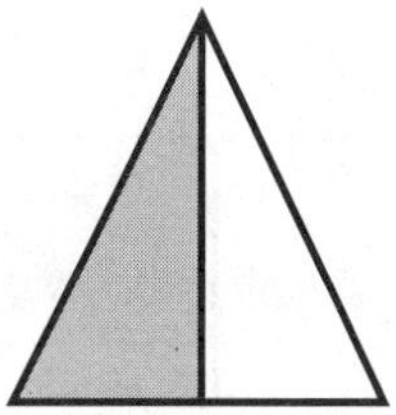

$\frac{\bigcirc}{2}$

4. 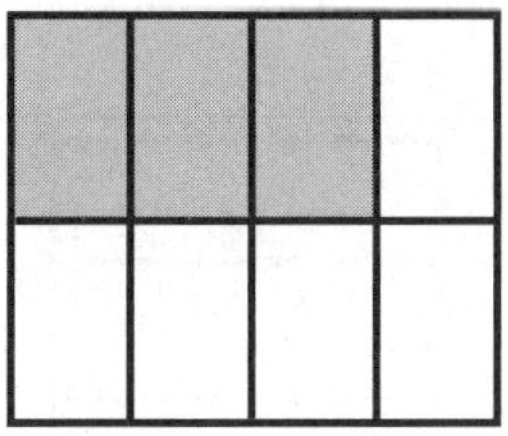

$\frac{\bigcirc}{8}$

5. 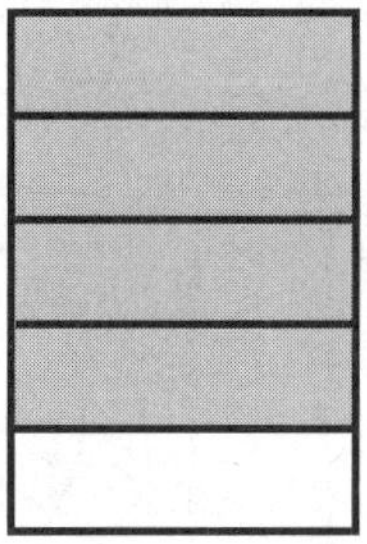

$\frac{\bigcirc}{5}$

6. 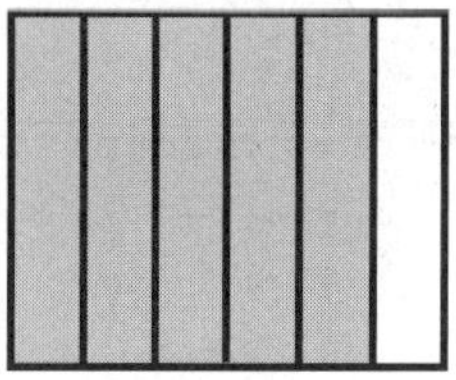

$\frac{\bigcirc}{6}$

Write the fraction that tells what part is shaded.

7. 

$\frac{3}{4}$

8. 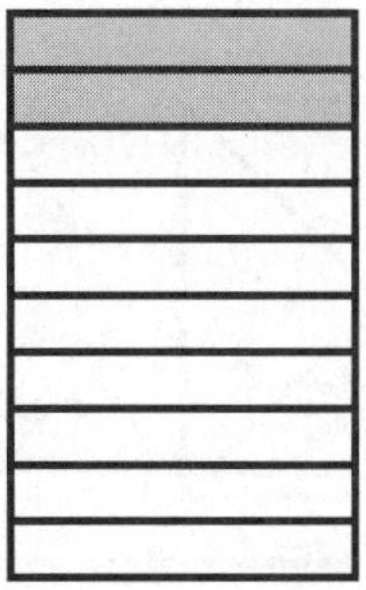

$\frac{\bigcirc}{\bigcirc}$

9. 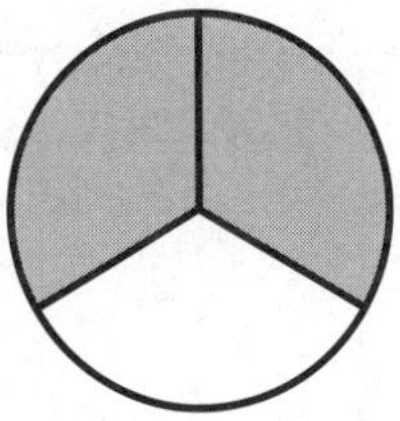

$\frac{\bigcirc}{\bigcirc}$

10. 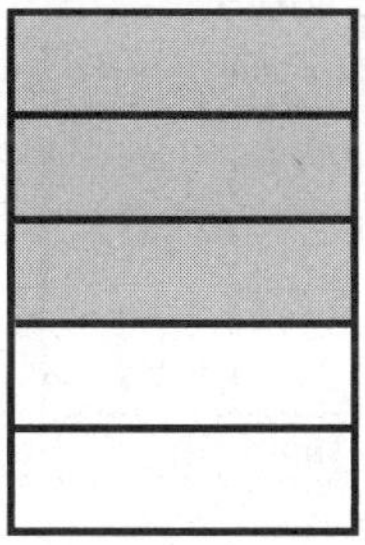

$\frac{\bigcirc}{\bigcirc}$

11. 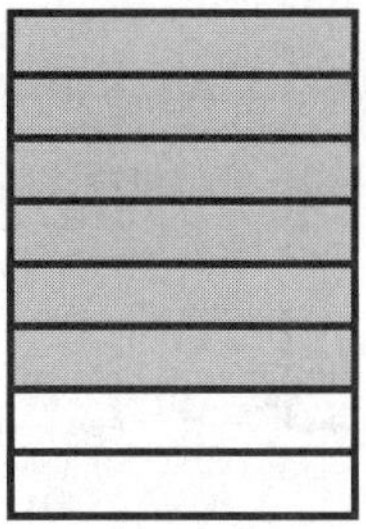

$\frac{\bigcirc}{\bigcirc}$

12. 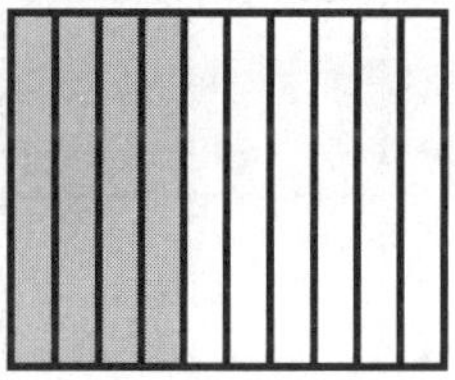

$\frac{\bigcirc}{\bigcirc}$

Name ______________________ Date ____________

COLORING FRACTIONS

Colorful Fractions

Follow the directions.

1. Color $\frac{1}{2}$.

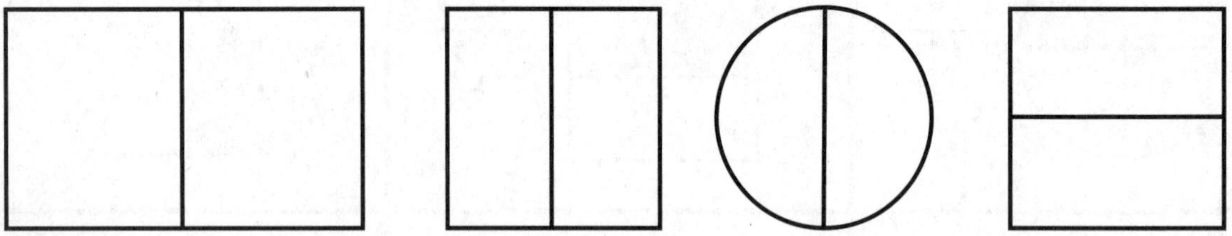

2. Color $\frac{1}{3}$.

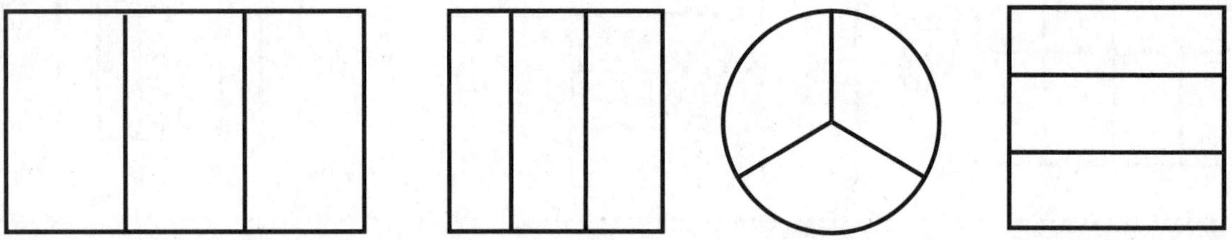

3. Color $\frac{1}{4}$.

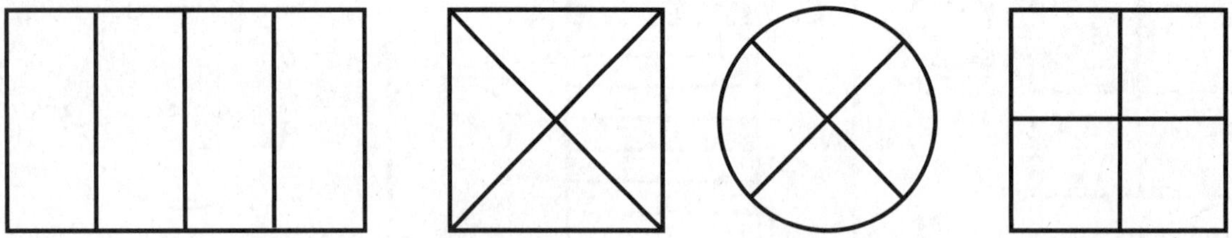

4. Color to show each fraction.

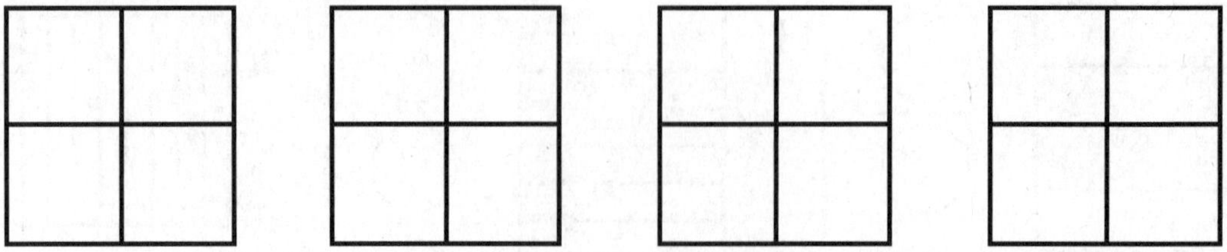

$\frac{1}{4}$ $\frac{2}{4}$ $\frac{3}{4}$ $\frac{4}{4}$

Name ______________________________ Date ________________

FINDING PARTS OF A GROUP

Pet Shop Fractions

Look at each picture. Answer the questions.

1.

What fraction of the cats have spots?

What fraction of the cats are white?

2.

What fraction of the dogs have long tails?

What fraction of the dogs have short tails?

3.

What fraction of the rabbits are sleeping?

What fraction of the rabbits are jumping?

4.

What fraction of the fish are small?

What fraction of the fish have stripes?

Name ______________________ Date ______________

SOLVING WORD PROBLEMS

Sweet Fractions

Read each story. Solve.

1. Some friends made a cake. Each friend got an equal part to decorate. Jen put raisins on her part. Linda put nuts on her part. Olga put coconut on her part. Draw a picture to show what part of the cake each friend decorated.

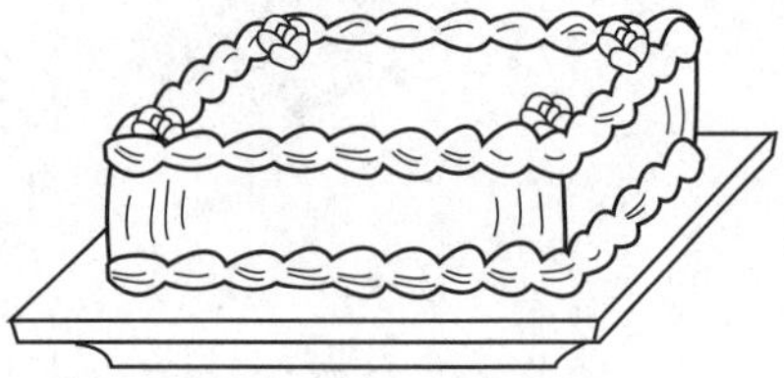

2. Sheila had 4 candles on a cake. She took off 3 candles. What part of the candles is left?

$\frac{\bigcirc}{\bigcirc}$ of the candles

3. Rico cut a pizza into 3 equal parts. What part did he eat? Circle the fraction.

$\frac{1}{2}$ $\frac{1}{3}$ $\frac{1}{4}$

4. Steve and Elena share a pie. Steve eats $\frac{1}{4}$ of the pie. Elena eats $\frac{2}{4}$ of the pie. How much of the pie is left? Circle the fraction.

$\frac{1}{4}$ $\frac{2}{4}$ $\frac{3}{4}$

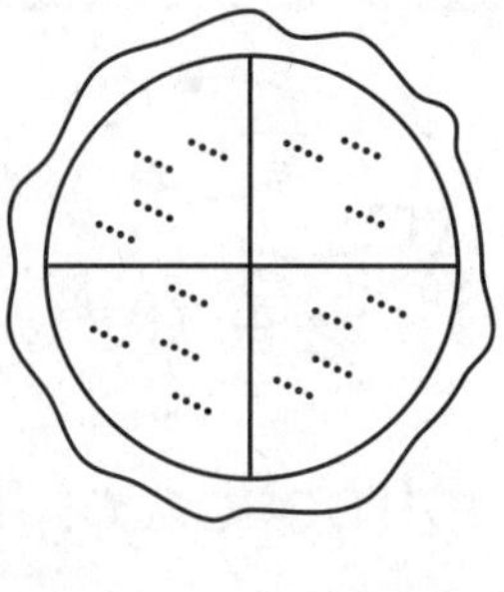

Name ______________________ Date ______________

Seeing Fractions

Follow the directions.

1. Look for 2 equal parts.
   Color them blue and red.

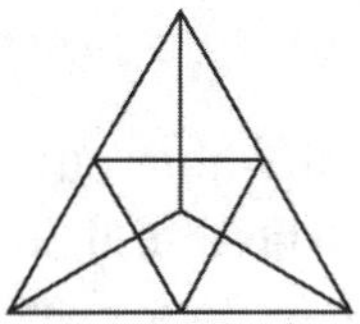

2. Look for 3 equal parts.
   Color them green,
   orange, and yellow.

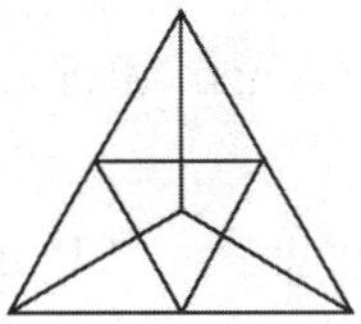

3. Look for 4 equal parts.
   Color them red, blue,
   yellow, and green.

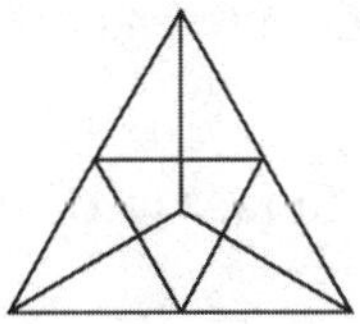

Name ______________________ Date ______________

Identifying Fraction Clocks

Look at each clock. Draw lines to match the words to the clock.

1. 

2. 

3. 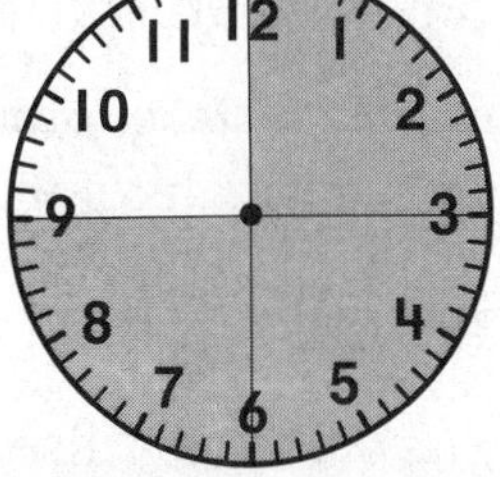

$\frac{1}{4}$ past the hour

$\frac{1}{2}$ past the hour

$\frac{3}{4}$ past the hour

Lesson 11

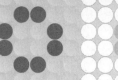

Length

Objective

- Develop a sense of whole numbers and represent and use them in flexible ways, including relating, composing, and decomposing numbers
- Relate ideas in geometry to ideas in number and measurement
- Recognize the attributes of length, volume, weight, area, and time
- Compare and order objects according to these attributes
- Understand how to measure using nonstandard and standard units
- Measure with multiple copies of units of the same size, such as paper clips laid end to end
- Use tools to measure
- Develop common referents for measures to make comparisons and estimates
- Apply and adapt a variety of appropriate strategies to solve problems

Vocabulary

centimeter—a unit of metric measure for length

inch—a unit of standard measure for length

perimeter—the distance around a figure found by adding the lengths of the sides

Materials

- connecting cubes, pencils, inch ruler, centimeter ruler, crayons, paper (optional), scissors (optional), desk items (optional), calculator (optional), number cubes (optional), craft paper (optional), markers (optional), yarn (optional)

Lesson Pages

Page 88 **(Manipulatives)**
Using connecting cubes, children estimate and measure ribbon.

Page 89 **(Practice)**
Children use an inch ruler to draw a line that shows how far a ladybug crawls.

Page 90 **(Practice)**
Children use a centimeter ruler to measure how far a snail crawls.

Page 91 **(Extension)**
Using a centimeter ruler, children measure how far bugs crawl and identify the one who goes the farthest.

Page 92 **(Word Problems)**
Children solve word problems about measuring.

Page 93 **(Enrichment)**
Activity Card 1: Children find the perimeter of six figures and color the ones whose perimeters are the same.
Activity Card 2: Children begin to understand map scale when they measure inches between items in a park and convert them to feet.

Another Look

- Cut paper strips in lengths from 1 inch to 12 inches. Have children order the strips and then measure them with an inch ruler. (Visual, Kinesthetic, ELL)
- Give pairs of children a centimeter ruler. Call out a measurement. Have children find things in their desk that are about the same length. (Visual, Kinesthetic, Auditory, ELL)

Extension

- Have children measure different objects in feet, such as desks or bookshelves. Then have them use a calculator to find the measurement in inches.
- Have partnered children each roll a number cube. Tell them to use their two cubes to make one number. Then give them a piece of craft paper. Tell them to draw two figures: one that has a perimeter with that number of centimeters and one that has a perimeter with that number of inches.

At Home

- Cut yarn that is 12 inches long and send it home. Have children measure things around the house to find those that are about the same length as the yarn ruler. Have them draw pictures to record their findings.
- Have children make paper centimeter rulers. Have them measure at least five things at home and record the measurements in a chart.
- Visit www.harcourtachieve.com/achievementzone for additional ideas and activity pages.

Answer Key

Page 88
Estimates will vary.
1. 5 **2.** 8
3. 3 **4.** 7

Page 89
Check that children draw a line to the correct inch length.

Page 90
1. 3 **2.** 7
3. 14 **4.** 6
5. 11

Page 91
snail: about 9 cm
ladybug: about 4 cm
centipede: about 7 cm
beetle: about 6 cm
turtle: about 8 cm
ant: about 3 cm
caterpillar: about 5 cm
Question: The snail went the farthest.

Page 92
1. Children draw a line to show 4 inches.
2. no
3. 24
4. no

Page 93
Card 1: Perimeters are 14, 19, and 22. Children color figures whose perimeters match the same color.
Card 2: Answers will vary.

Name ______________________ Date ______________

UNDERSTANDING MEASUREMENT

Guess and Measure

How long is each ribbon? Write an estimate. Then use cubes to check your measurement.

1. 

Estimate
about ______ cubes

Measure
______ cubes

2. 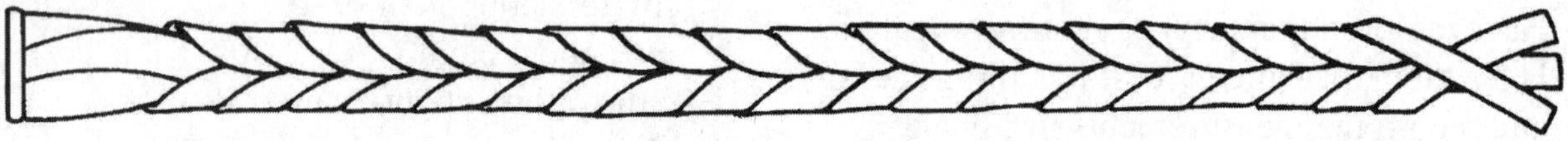

Estimate
about ______ cubes

Measure
______ cubes

3. 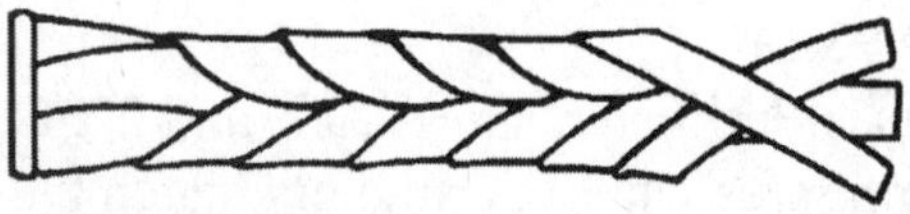

Estimate
about ______ cubes

Measure
______ cubes

4. 

Estimate
about ______ cubes

Measure
______ cubes

Name ______________________ Date ____________

MEASURING WITH INCHES

Going Buggy

Use an inch ruler. Draw a line to show how far each ladybug crawls.

1. 

2 inches

---

2. 

5 inches

---

3. 

1 inch

---

4. 

6 inches

---

5. 

3 inches

Name ______________________________ Date ________________

MEASURING WITH CENTIMETERS

A Slow and Steady Measure

Use a centimeter ruler. Measure how far each snail crawls.

1.

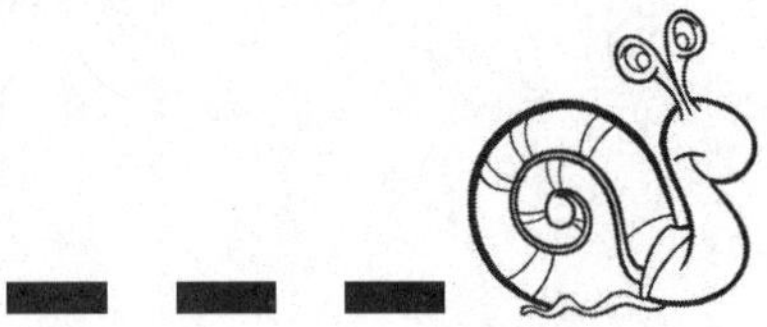

_______ centimeters

2.

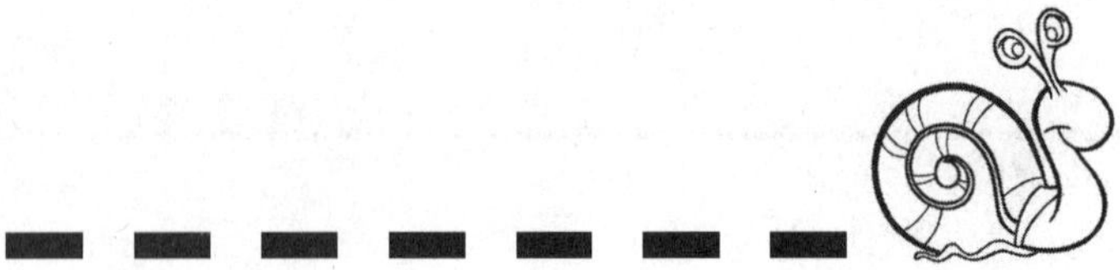

_______ centimeters

3.

_______ centimeters

4.

_______ centimeters

5.

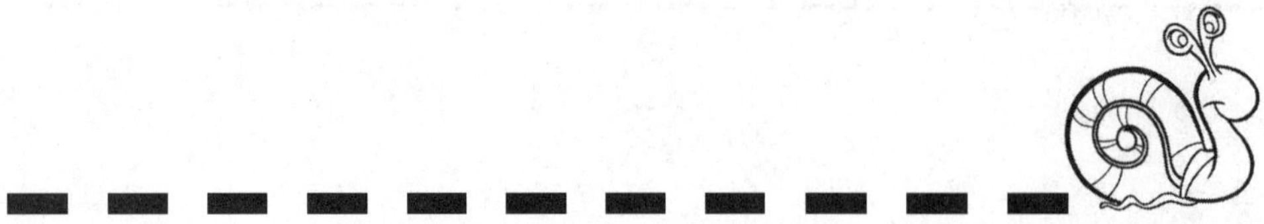

_______ centimeters

Name ______________________________ Date ______________

PRACTICING MEASUREMENT

How Far Did They Go?

How far did each animal go? Estimate. Then use a centimeter ruler to measure. Write the answer.

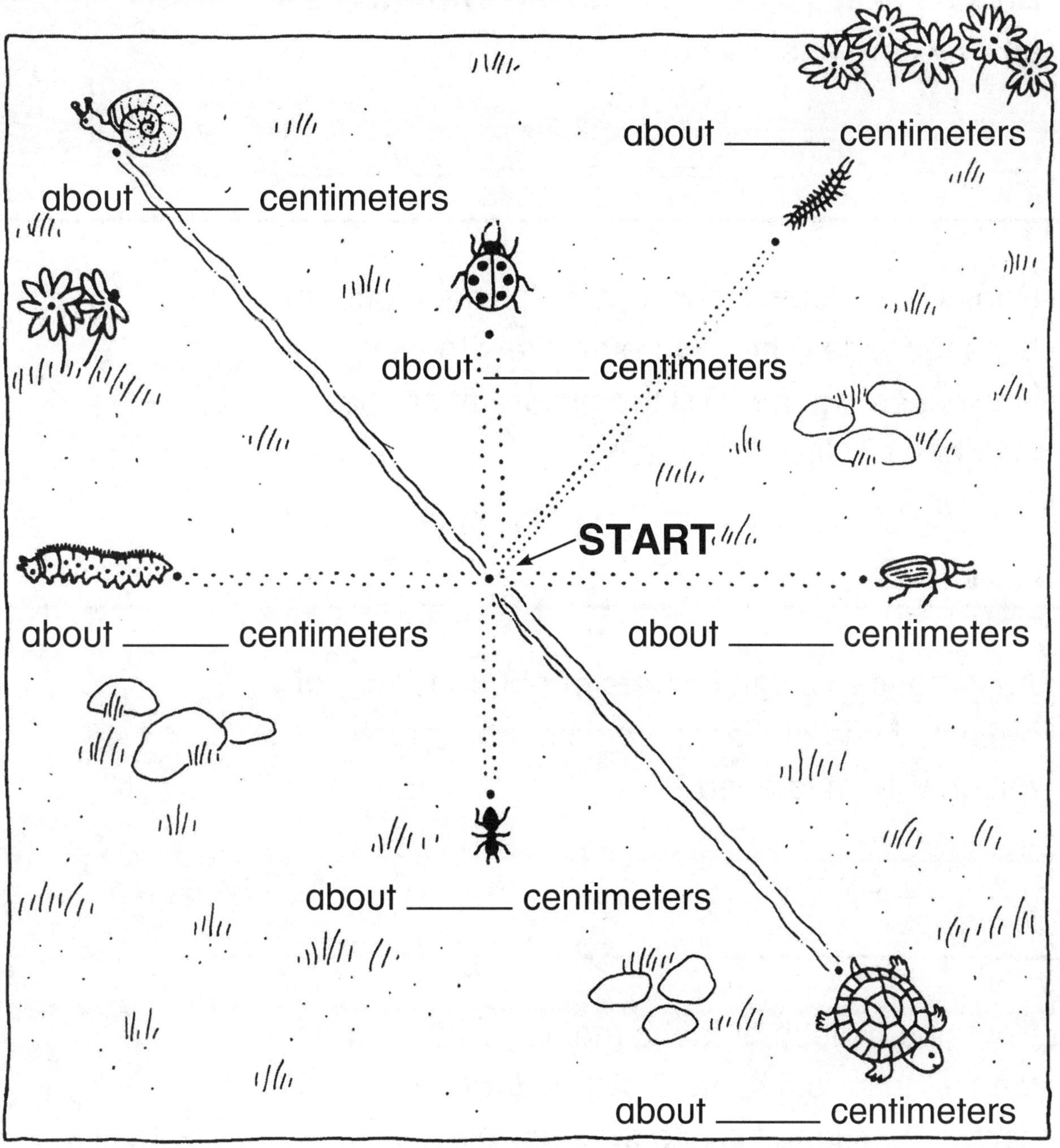

Who went the farthest? ______________________________

Name ______________________________ Date ______________

SOLVING WORD PROBLEMS

Measuring is "Sew" Much Fun!

Read each story. Solve.

1. Rhonda needs 4 inches of ribbon. Draw a line to show where she will cut.

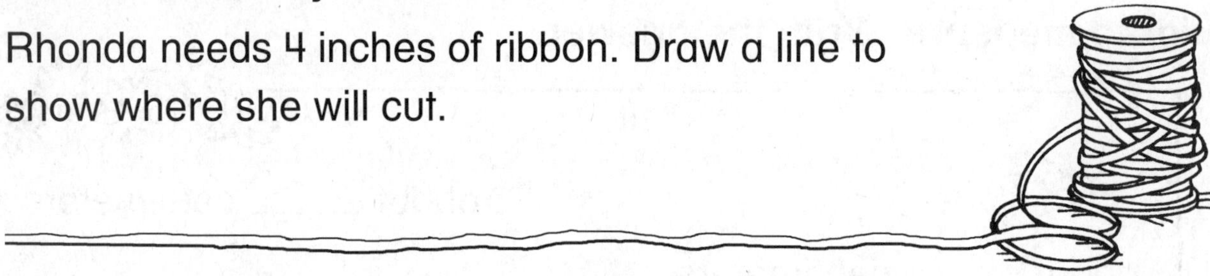

2. Daniel has a quilt block that is 7 inches long and 8 inches wide. The picture he drew to sew on it is 8 inches square. Will the picture fit on the quilt block? Circle the answer.

yes no

3. Anita needs 12 centimeters of ribbon for a craft project. If she makes 2 projects, how much ribbon will Anita need?

________ cm

4. Paul has a piece of fabric that is 16 centimeters long. Can he cut it into 2 pieces that are 9 centimeters long? Circle the answer.

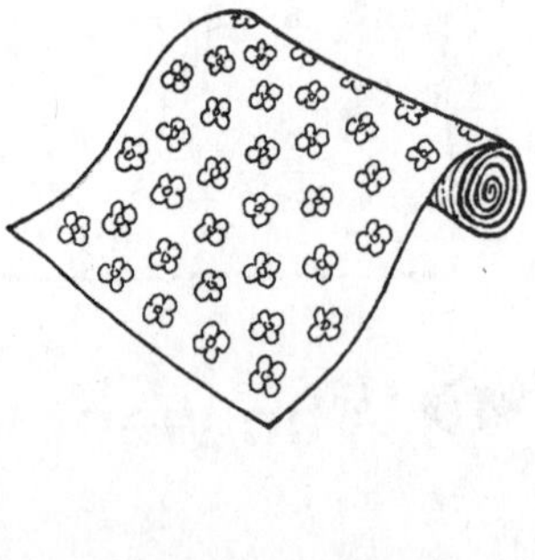

yes no

Name ______________________ Date ____________

Measuring Perimeter

➔ **Find each perimeter. Write the perimeter inside the figure. Color the figures with matching perimeters the same color.**

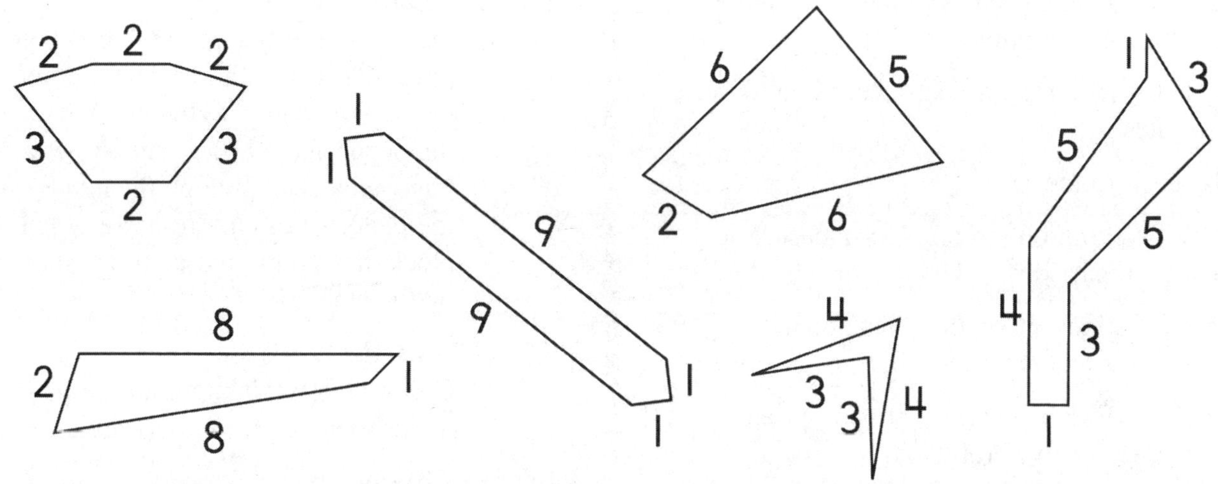

Name ______________________ Date ____________

Mapping It Out

➔ **A scale shows distance on a map. Look at the scale on this map. Use the scale and your inch ruler. Write how many feet there are between five different places. Round your answer to the nearest 100 feet.**

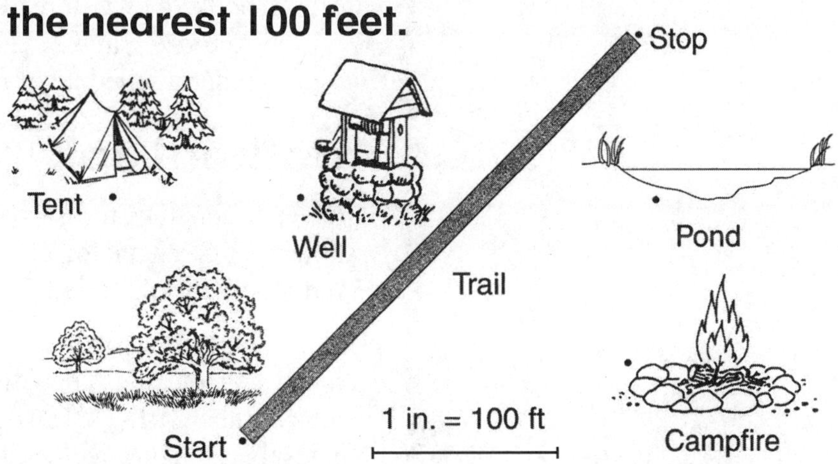

Lesson 12

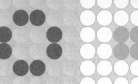

Time

Objectives

- Recognize the attributes of length, volume, weight, area, and time
- Compare and order objects according to these attributes
- Use tools to measure
- Develop common referents for measures to make comparisons and estimates
- Pose questions and gather data about themselves and their surroundings
- Apply and adapt a variety of appropriate strategies to solve problems

Vocabulary

analog—a clock that uses an hour hand and a minute hand to show the time

digital—a clock that uses numbers to show the time

Materials

- Analog Clock (page 127), paper plates, fasteners, scissors, pencils, masking tape or chalk (optional), index cards (optional), number cube (optional)

Lesson Pages

Page 96 **(Manipulatives)**
Duplicate the analog clock parts on page 127. Have children cut out the clock parts and glue the clock face on the paper plate. Show them how to push a fastener through the hands and the plate. After children assemble the clock, have them model times shown on the clocks and write the times.

Page 97 **(Practice)**
Children draw the hour and minute hands to show times to the quarter hour.

Page 98 **(Practice)**
Children estimate if specified activities take about 1 minute or 1 hour.

Page 99 **(Extension)**
Children draw a line to show the feeding schedule of animals at a zoo. Times advance in increments of fifteen minutes.

Page 100 **(Word Problems)**
Children read stories and solve time problems.

Page 101 **(Enrichment)**
Activity Card 1: Children plan the books they will read on a cassette tape.
Activity Card 2: Using logic, children order a schedule of given events.

Another Look

- Have partners take turns saying a time and showing it on an analog clock. (Visual, Auditory, Kinesthetic, ELL)
- Make a tape circle on the floor or draw a chalk circle outside. Then distribute large cards numbered 1–12. Have children arrange themselves to show a clock face. Ask 2

additional children to be the hour and minute hands on the clock. Name a time to the hour and have children holding those cards say, "Tick tock." The "hands" point to the appropriate number, too. Repeat the activity so that each child can participate. (Visual, Kinesthetic, Auditory, ELL)

Extension

- Invite children to choose a favorite food to cook or bake. Have them write a time schedule from start to finish to show how long it will take to prepare the food.
- Provide partners with an analog clock and a number cube. Partners take turns showing a clock time. The other partner rolls a number on the cube and tells the time that number of hours later.

At Home

- Have children create a time schedule to show the television programs they watch and the times the programs stop and start. Ask children to bring the schedules to class. Help them add the total number of minutes they watched television.
- Invite children to cut out pictures of familiar activities, such as eating or sleeping, from recycled magazines. Have children label each activity with a time that someone might do the activity. Then have them order their pictures from morning to night.
- Visit www.harcourtachieve.com/achievementzone for additional ideas and activity pages.

Answer Key

Page 96

1. 4:00	**2.** 12:00	**3.** 2:30
4. 9:30	**5.** 6:30	**6.** 1:15
7. 5:45	**8.** 3:15	

Page 97

Children draw clock hands to show these times:

1. 5:00	**2.** 7:15	**3.** 12:30
4. 9:45	**5.** 1:30	**6.** 3:45
7. 2:00	**8.** 8:30	**9.** 11:15

Page 98

1. 1 minute	**2.** 1 hour	**3.** 1 minute
4. 1 hour	**5.** 1 hour	**6.** 1 minute

Page 99

Answers advance in increments of 15 minutes: zebra 10:15, bear 10:30, monkey 10:45, rhino 11:00, ducks 11:15, peacock 11:30, panther 11:45, eagle 12:00

Page 100

1. Children draw hands to show 7:45.
2. 1 minute
3. 10:30
4. 11:30

Page 101

Card 1: Answers will vary.
Card 2:
9:00–10:00: Math
10:00–12:00: Reading
12:30–1:30: Science
1:30–2:00: Writing
2:00–3:00: Music

Name ______________________ Date ______________

UNDERSTANDING TIME TO THE QUARTER HOUR

Around the Clock

Show the time on the clock. Write the time.

1. 

____

2. 

____

3. 

____

4. 

____

5. 

____

6. 

____

7. 

____

8. 

____

Name ______________________________ Date ________________

WRITING TIME

Time on Our Hands

Draw the hour hand and minute hand to show each time.

1.

2.

3.

4.

5.

6.

7.

8.

9.

Name ______________________________ Date ______________

ESTIMATING TIME

How Long?

About how long does each activity take? Circle the better estimate.

1.

to drink a glass of water

I minute   I hour

2.

to play a game

I minute   I hour

3.

to yawn

I minute   I hour

4.

to cook dinner

I minute   I hour

5.

to shop for clothes

I minute   I hour

6.

to wash your face

I minute   I hour

Name ______________________ Date ______________

UNDERSTANDING TIME ORDER

Time to Feed

The zookeeper feeds an animal every 15 minutes. Draw a line to show her path from 10:15 until her lunch break at 12:00.

START

FINISH

Name ____________________ Date ____________

SOLVING WORD PROBLEMS

School Time

Read each story. Solve.

1. School starts at 7:45. Draw the hands on the clock to show the time.

2. The teacher asks the children to get in line. About how long will it take? Circle the answer.

1 minute   1 hour

3. Look at the clock. It is time for math. What time is it?

_______:_______

4. Look at the clock in problem 3. The class is going on a bus ride to the zoo. The bus leaves the school in 1 hour. What time will the bus leave?

_______:_______

Name ______________________ Date ______________

Reading Time

Your teacher gives you a thirty-minute cassette tape. You are to choose your favorite books to record on the tape. Which books will you choose? How many books can you record on the tape?

Book Title	Time

Name ______________________ Date ______________

Scheduling Time for School

Read the sentences. Complete the schedule.

1. Music begins at 2:00.
2. Reading is from 10:00 to 12:00.
3. Science begins 30 minutes after reading ends.
4. Math ends at 10:00.
5. Writing lasts 30 minutes.

9:00–10:00	10:00–12:00	12:30–1:30	1:30–2:00	2:00–3:00

Lesson 13

Money

Objectives

- Count with understanding and recognize "how many" in sets of objects
- Develop a sense of whole numbers and represent and use them in flexible ways, including relating, composing, and decomposing numbers
- Connect number words and numerals to the quantities they represent, using various physical models and representations
- Understand various meanings of addition and subtraction of whole numbers and the relationship between the two operations
- Understand the effects of adding and subtracting whole numbers
- Develop and use strategies for whole-number computations, with a focus on addition and subtraction
- Develop fluency with basic number combinations for addition and subtraction
- Use a variety of methods and tools to compute, including objects, mental computation, estimation, paper and pencil, and calculators
- Develop common referents for measures to make comparisons and estimates
- Apply and adapt a variety of appropriate strategies to solve problems

Vocabulary

bill—paper money

cent—the smallest value of currency in the United States

coin—metal money

dime—a coin with a value of ten cents

dollar—the accepted currency in the United States

half dollar—a coin with a value of fifty cents

nickel—a coin with a value of five cents

penny—a coin with a value of one cent

quarter—a coin with a value of twenty-five cents

Materials

- coin manipulatives, pencils, calculator, crayons, envelopes (optional), index cards (optional), toy pictures from recycled magazines and newspaper ads (optional), price tags (optional), glue (optional)

Lesson Pages

Page 104 (Manipulatives)
Using coin manipulatives, children find different ways to show the amounts. Then they trace the fewest coins to show each amount.

Page 105 (Practice)
Children color the coins needed to buy treats.

Page 106 (Practice)
Children draw lines to the bills and coins needed to buy tools. Then they write the values from the least to the greatest.

Page 107 (Extension)
Children find the values of groups of coins and use a calculator to find the sum. Then they use the amounts to move through a puzzle to find out what Leo bought.

Page 108 (Word Problems)
Children solve word problems about money.

Page 109 (Enrichment)
Activity Card 1: Children complete a chart to show how many of each coin are needed to make $1.00.

Activity Card 2: Children make a list to show 3 ways they can spend $1.00 at a bake sale.

Another Look

- Show each kind of coin. Have children count out the number of pennies to show the amount. (Visual, Kinesthetic, ELL)
- Place a variety of coins in envelopes. Write the values of the coins on separate cards. Then invite partners to choose an envelope, count the coins, and choose the correct card. While they are sorting the coins, have partners look at and describe the coins according to color, size, pictures, and numbers they see. (Visual, Auditory)

Extension

- Cut out toy pictures from recycled magazines or newspaper ads. Make price tags up to 99¢ to glue to them. Then tell children to imagine they have $1.00. Have them figure out the change they will get back after "buying" single items or groups of items.
- Children get a handful of coins and find the value. Then they trade to find the least number of coins they can have.

At Home

- Suggest that children go shopping with a family member. Challenge them to count out the bills and coins needed to pay the total amount.
- Ask children to look at an old sales receipt and find two items that cost less than $3.00. Then have them draw the bills and coins to show each amount.
- Visit www.harcourtachieve.com/achievementzone for additional ideas and activity pages.

Answer Key

Page 104
Children trace the following coins:
1. 1 dime and 3 pennies
2. 1 quarter, 1 nickel, and 2 pennies
3. 2 quarters, 1 dime, and 1 nickel
4. 3 quarters and 1 nickel

Page 105
Children color the following coins:
1. 1 dime, 1 nickel, and 1 penny
2. 1 quarter and 3 pennies
3. 1 quarter, 1 nickel, and 2 pennies
4. 1 quarter and 1 dime
5. 1 quarter, 1 dime, 1 nickel, and 3 pennies

Page 106

1. c	**2.** e	**3.** a
4. d	**5.** b	**6.** $1.37
7. $1.56	**8.** $1.95	**9.** $2.40
10. $2.75		

Page 107

1. 41	**2.** 56	**3.** 90
4. 37	**5.** 27	**6.** 85
7. $3.36		

Leo bought a book.

Page 108

1. 55	**2.** 3 pennies
3. no	**4.** 51¢

Page 109
Card 1:
half dollar: 2
quarter: 4
dime: 10
nickel: 20
penny: 100
Card 2: Answers will vary.

Name ______________________ Date ______________

UNDERSTANDING COIN VALUES

Coin Counts

Work with a partner. Find different ways to show the amount. Trace the way that shows the least number of coins.

1.

2.

3.

4.

Name ______________________________ Date ________________

PRACTICING COUNTING COINS

Sweet Treats

➜ **Color the coins you need to buy each treat.**

1.

2.

3.

4.

5.

Name ______________________ Date ______________

PRACTICING COUNTING BILLS AND COINS

Tool Time

Draw lines to match the tool with its amount.

1. 

a. 

2. 

b. 

3. 

c. 

4. 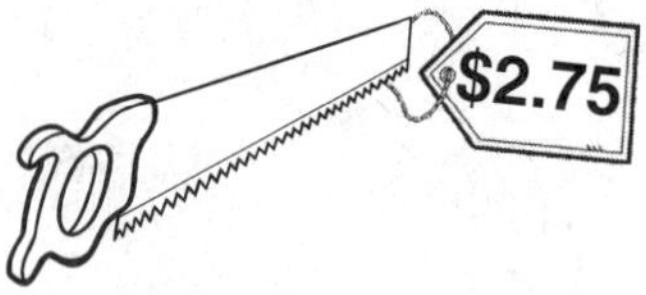

d. 

5. 

e. 

Write the amounts from above in order from least to greatest.

6. ________ 7. ________

8. ________ 9. ________ 10. ________

Name ______________________________ Date _______________

ADDING GROUPS OF COINS

Making Money

Leo did some jobs. How much money did he earn? Write the amounts. Then answer the question.

1. 

__________¢

2. 

__________¢

3. 

__________¢

4. 

__________¢

5. 

__________¢

6. 

__________¢

7. How much did Leo earn altogether?

Use a calculator. ____________________

Leo went to the store. What did he buy? Follow the path using the amounts in the order above.

41¢	56¢	72¢	35¢
21¢	90¢	37¢	59¢
63¢	58¢	27¢	85¢

 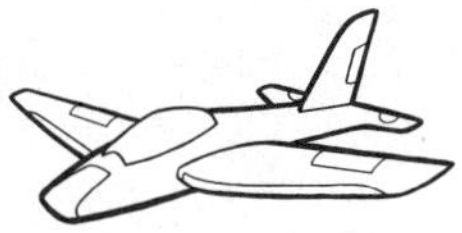 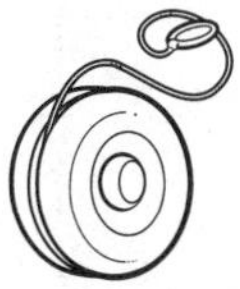 

Name ______________________________ Date ______________

SOLVING WORD PROBLEMS

The Problem with Money

Read each problem. Solve.

1. Mae has 1 quarter and 4 nickels in her bank. She adds 1 dime. How much money does Mae have in her bank now?

__________¢

2. Tran has 58¢ in all. She takes out the coins shown here. What coins does she have left in her purse? Circle the coin name. Write how many.

__________ dimes nickels pennies

3. Allan has these coins.

Does he have enough to buy a flashlight? Circle the answer.

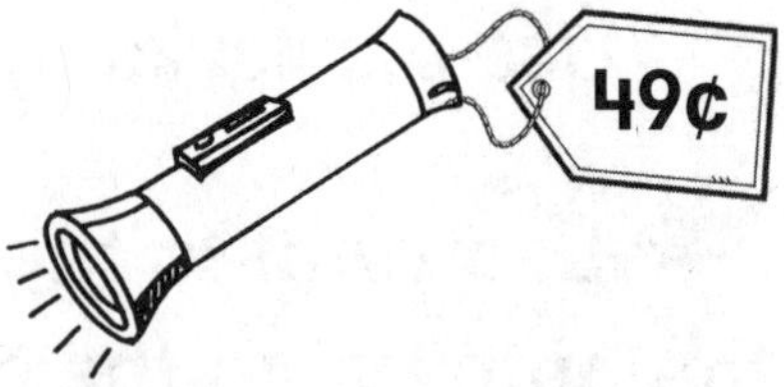

yes no

4. Which amount could you make with the least number of coins? Circle the answer.

41¢ 51¢ 61¢

Name ______________________ Date ______________

Making a Dollar

$1.00

Write how many of each coin you need to make $1.00.

Name ______________________ Date ______________

Buying at a Bake Sale

You have $1.00. What will you buy? List 3 ways you can spend the money.

50¢

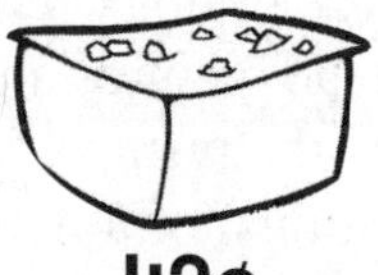
42¢

55¢

25¢

65¢

30¢

1. ______________________________

2. ______________________________

3. ______________________________

Lesson 14

Bar Graphs

Objectives

- Count with understanding and recognize "how many" in sets of objects
- Develop a sense of whole numbers and represent and use them in flexible ways, including relating, composing, and decomposing numbers
- Pose questions and gather data about themselves and their surroundings
- Sort and classify objects according to their attributes and organize data about the objects
- Represent data using concrete objects, pictures, and graphs
- Describe parts of the data and the set of data as a whole to determine what the data show
- Apply and adapt a variety of appropriate strategies to solve problems

Vocabulary

bar graph—a graph that uses bars to show how many

scale—the numbers along the side or bottom of the graph that show how many

tally—a straight mark made for one thing that is counted

Materials

- red, blue, and yellow connecting cubes; crayons; pencils; construction paper in a variety of colors (optional); pattern blocks (optional); books on a shelf (optional); one-inch graph paper (optional)

Lesson Pages

Page 112 (Manipulatives)
To develop an understanding of bar graphs, children use connecting cubes to count colors of gumballs in a picture.

Page 113 (Practice)
Children count shapes in a picture and record the data in a chart using both tallies and numbers. Then they color the boxes to complete a graph.

Page 114 (Practice)
Children answer questions about a bar graph.

Page 115 (Extension)
Children use logic to answer questions about pets children have. Then they complete a chart and bar graph.

Page 116 (Word Problems)
Children solve word problems about a graph.

Page 117 (Enrichment)
Activity Card 1: Children poll classmates and make a graph about favorite kinds of pizza.
Activity Card 2: Children look at a picture of dogs. They find one way to sort the pictures and make a graph to show the results. Then they write three questions for a friend to answer about the graph.

Another Look

- Have partners get a handful of different colors of connecting cubes. Tell them to make trains with cubes that are the same color. Have them align the left ends of the trains. Ask questions that help children understand how the cubes make a graph. (Kinesthetic, Visual, Auditory, ELL)

- Lay out a variety of colors of construction paper. Invite each child to choose his or her favorite color of paper and write a name on it. Help children create a large graph on the floor showing their favorite colors. Discuss the importance of a title and the scale as you add it to the graph. (Visual, Kinesthetic, ELL)

Extension

- Invite partners to make a picture or a design with pattern blocks. Have them trade pictures with a partner and show the data using a chart and graph. Challenge partners to take turns asking questions about the graphs.
- Have children sort the books on a shelf into genre categories. Then have them chart and graph the results.

At Home

- Ask children to take a walk with a family member and use tallies to count the animals they see. Have them make a graph to show the data when they return home. Ask them to write three questions about the graph.
- Give each child a sheet of 1-inch graph paper. Have them make a graph to show the length of the name of each person in the family.
- Visit www.harcourtachieve.com/achievementzone for additional ideas and activity pages.

Answer Key

Page 112
Children color boxes to show the following colors: **red**-4; **blue**-5; **yellow**-3

Page 113
Our Funny Bird Chart
circle: 2 tallies; 2
square: 4 tallies; 4
rectangle: 5 tallies; 5
triangle: 7 tallies; 7
Our Funny Bird Graph
Children color the following boxes:
circle: 2
square: 4
rectangle: 5
triangle: 7

Page 114
1. apple **2.** banana
3. orange and grapes **4.** 4
5. 18

Page 115
Dog: 5 tallies **Cat:** 4 tallies
Turtle: 1 tally **Bird:** 3 tallies
Fish: 2 tallies
Children color the following boxes:
Dog-5 **Cat**-4
Turtle-1 **Bird**-3
Fish-2

Page 116
1. chocolate
2. lemon
3. $10 - 3 = 7$; 7 cakes
4. $7 + 5 = 12$; 12 cakes
5. $10 + 7 + 3 + 5 = 25$; 25 cakes

Page 117
Card 1: Answers will vary.
Card 2: Answers will vary.

Name ______________________ Date ______________

UNDERSTANDING A BAR GRAPH

Gumball Graphing

➜ **Put a cube on each gumball to show the color. Join cubes that are the same color. Color a square in the graph for each cube of the same color.**

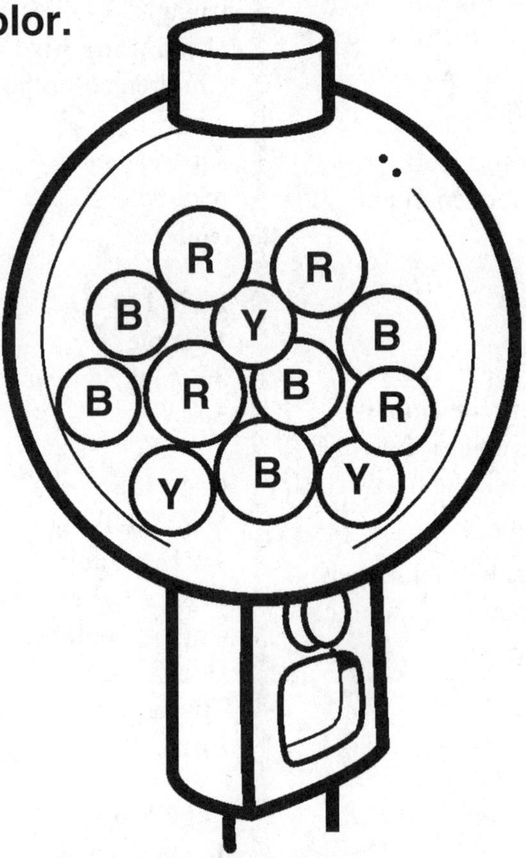

Gumballs					
Red					
Yellow					
Blue					

Name ______________________________ Date ______________

MAKING A CHART AND GRAPH

Shape Sort

➜ **Some children made this picture with pattern blocks. How many of each shape did they use? Complete the table.**

Our Funny Bird Chart		
Shape	**Tally**	**Number**
○		
□		
▯		
△		

➜ **Use the chart. Color a box in the graph for each shape.**

Our Funny Bird Graph										
○										
□										
▯										
△										

Name ______________________ Date ______________

READING A GRAPH

Favorite Fruits

➜ **Look at the graph. Then answer the questions.**

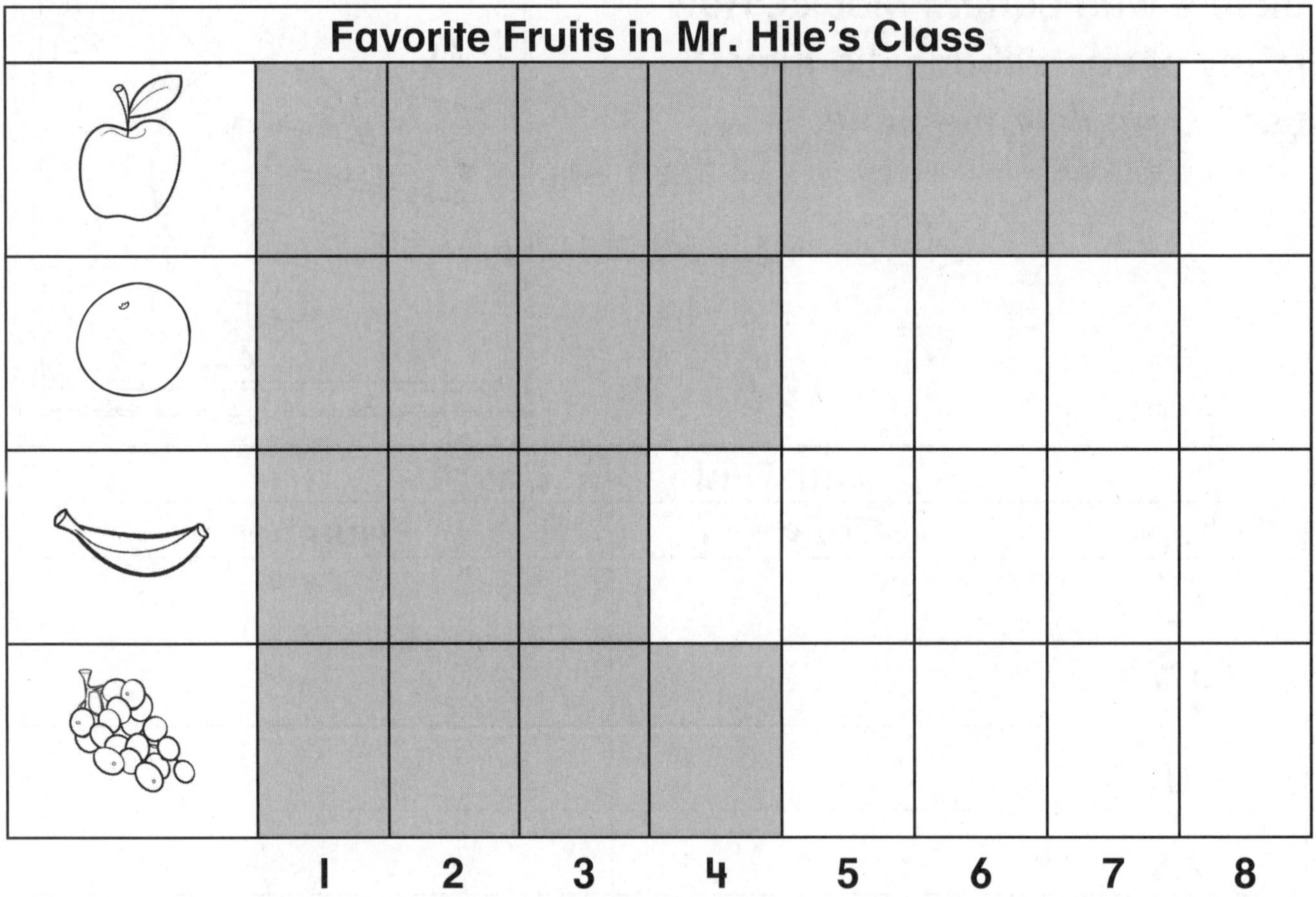

1. Which fruit did the most children like? ______________

2. Which fruit was the least favorite? ______________

3. Which fruits got the same number of votes? ______________

4. How many more children liked apples than bananas? ______________

5. How many children are in Mr. Hile's class? ______________

Name ______________________ Date ____________

PRACTICING GRAPHING SKILLS

Picture This Graph

Read the statements. Then complete the table using tally marks.

1. Only one child has a turtle.
2. Twice as many children have fish as turtles.
3. Two more children have birds rather than turtles.
4. Five children have dogs.
5. The number of children who have cats is one less than those who have dogs.

Pets	Tally
Dog	
Cat	
Turtle	
Bird	
Fish	

Use the chart. Color a box in the graph to show the number of children who have each kind of pet.

Pets								
Dog								
Cat								
Turtle								
Bird								
Fish								
	1	2	3	4	5	6	7	8

Name ______________________ Date ______________

SOLVING WORD PROBLEMS

The Problem with Cakes

A bakery made a graph to show the cakes it sold in one week. Look at the graph. Then answer the questions.

1. Which cake did the most people buy? ______________________

2. Which cake did the fewest people buy? ______________________

3. How many more people bought chocolate cake than lemon cake? Write the number sentence.

   ______________________ __________ cakes

4. How many people bought vanilla and pineapple cakes? Write the number sentence.

   ______________________ __________ cakes

5. How many cakes did the bakery sell in all that week? Write the number sentence.

   ______________________ __________ cakes

Name ______________________________ Date ______________

Asking and Graphing

➡ What kind of pizza do your friends like? Ask 10 people. Make a tally mark for each vote. Then make a graph on another sheet of paper to show the votes.

Kinds of Pizza	Tally	Number

Name ______________________________ Date ______________

Making a Graph from a Picture

➡ Look at the dogs. Make a graph on another sheet of paper to show how many of each. Write 3 questions about the graph. Give the graph and the questions to a friend to answer.

Lesson 15

Probability

Objectives

- Sort and classify objects according to their attributes and organize data about the objects
- Represent data using concrete objects, pictures, and graphs
- Describe parts of the data and the set of data as a whole to determine what the data show
- Discuss events related to students' experiences as likely or unlikely
- Apply and adapt a variety of appropriate strategies to solve problems

Vocabulary

probability—the chance of an event happening

Materials

- paper clips, pencils, blue and red connecting cubes, small brown bags, yellow connecting cubes (optional), pennies (optional), construction paper (optional), scissors (optional), recycled envelopes (optional)

Lesson Pages

Page 120 (Manipulatives)
To develop an understanding of probability, children compare the outcome of spinning a paper clip 20 times on two different spinners. One spinner has equal divisions of black and white. The second spinner has more black than white.

Page 121 (Practice)
Children answer questions and practice predicting outcomes based on the number of colored items in a bag.

Page 122 (Practice)
Children begin to understand possible outcomes based on variables when they make a list to record all the ways that three cards can land.

Page 123 (Extension)
Placing 7 blue cubes and 3 red cubes in a bag, partners take turns pulling out the cubes and recording the colors.

Page 124 (Word Problems)
Children solve word problems to show an understanding of probability.

Page 125 (Enrichment)
Activity Card 1: Children explore probability using different variables.
Activity Card 2: Children explore how to make a fair game board that is divided into 4 parts.

Another Look

- Join connecting cubes to make 8 pattern trains. Put them on separate pieces of construction paper. Include 2 more cubes, one of which will come next in the pattern. Have children add the cube that will most likely come next. (Visual, Kinesthetic, ELL)

- Give partners a penny. Have them predict if heads or tails will result most often in coin tosses. Ask partners to take turns flipping the coin to check their guess. Help them record the results in a chart with tally marks. (Visual, Kinesthetic, ELL)

Extension

- Have children repeat the cube activity on page 123, but this time add 3 yellow cubes.
- Have children figure out the possible outcomes using two spinners that have equal divisions of red, yellow, and blue colors.

At Home

- Have children cut out 4 blue, 2 yellow, and 1 red square from paper and store them in recycled envelopes. Have them take the squares home and ask a family member to predict the color that will be pulled out most often. Tell children to check the guess by pulling out a square 20 times. Remind them to use tally marks to record the results.
- Have children look at the board games they have at home to see how the board is divided to make it fair. Have them share their findings with the class. Discuss why it is important to have games that are fair.
- Visit <u>www.harcourtachieve.com/achievementzone</u> for additional ideas and activity pages.

Answer Key

Page 120
Answers will vary.

Page 121

1. 5	**2.** 3	**3.** 2
4. black	**5.** black	**6.** white
7. white	**8.** white	**9.** black
10. white	**11.** white	**12.** white
13. black		

Page 122
Answer order may vary.

1. 2 triangles and 1 circle
2. 1 triangle and 2 circles
3. 3 circles
4. 3 triangles

Page 123

1. blue and red
2. Answers will vary.
3. Answers will vary.
4. There were more blue cubes than red cubes.

Page 124

1. Children draw a spinner that is no more than $\frac{1}{4}$ red.
2. Children circle the first spinner with mostly black.
3. white

Page 125
Card 1: Answer order may vary.
red, red
red, red
red, yellow
blue, red
blue, red
blue, yellow
Card 2:

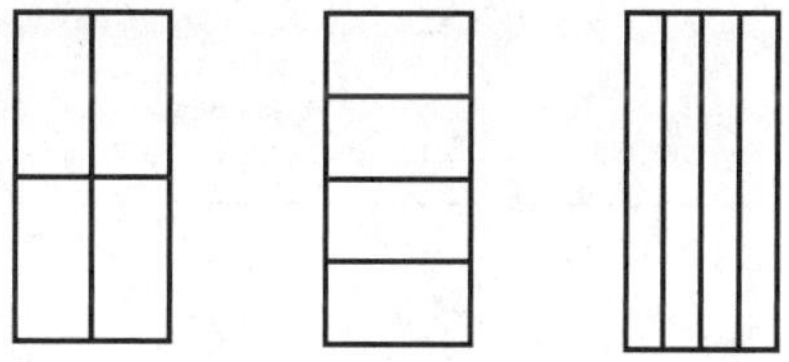

Name ______________________ Date ____________

UNDERSTANDING PROBABILITY

Spinning Games

Which spinner will stop on black more often? Circle A or B. Then use a pencil and a paper clip to make a spinner. Spin the clip 20 times on each spinner. Make a tally mark after each spin.

A.

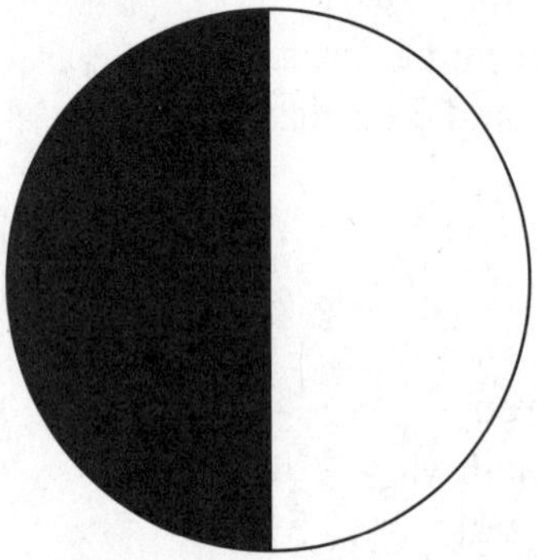

B.

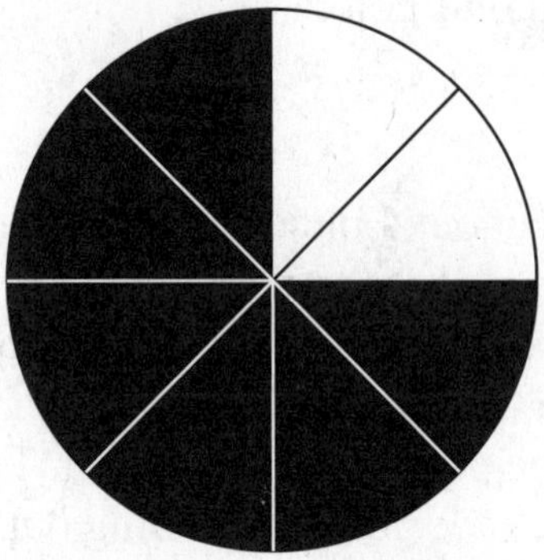

Color	Tally	Total
Black		
White		

Color	Tally	Total
Black		
White		

Answer the questions.

1. Was your guess correct? ______________________

____

2. Tell what happened. ______________________

____

____

Name ______________________ Date ______________

EXPLORING PROBABILITY

Most Likely Marbles

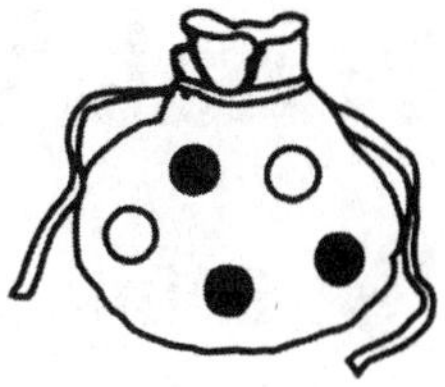

Look at the bag. Answer the questions.

1. How many marbles are in the bag? ______________
2. How many marbles are black? ______________
3. How many marbles are white? ______________
4. Are there more white or black marbles? ______________
5. Which color are you more likely to pull out from the bag? ______

Write the color you would be more likely to pull out from each bag.

6. 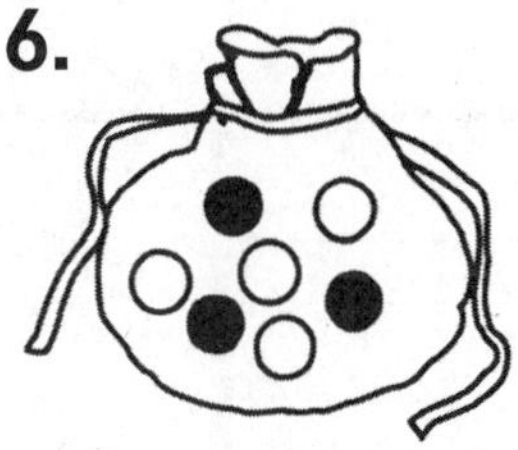

______

7. 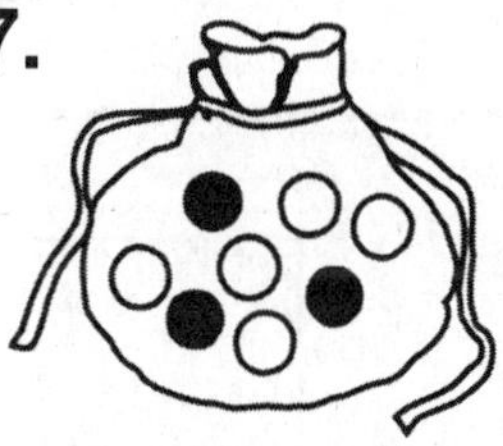

______

8. 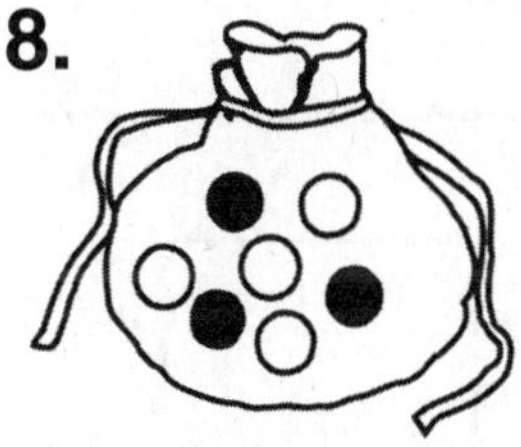

______

9. 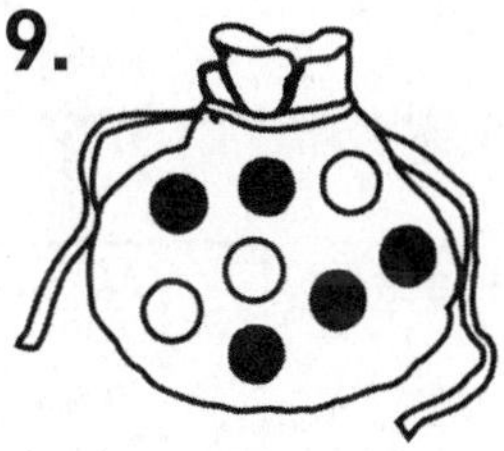

______

10. 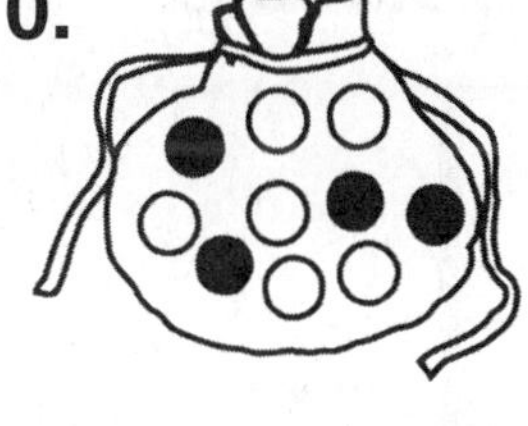

______

11. 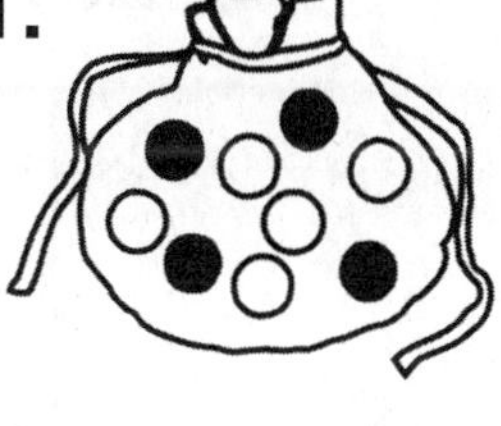

______

12. 

______

13. 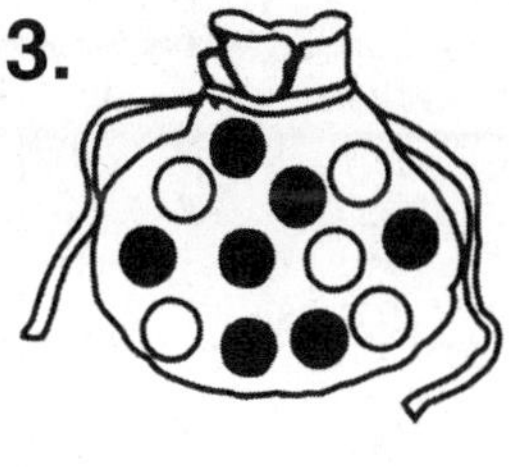

______

Name ____________________ Date ____________

EXPLORING POSSIBLE OUTCOMES

What Will Happen?

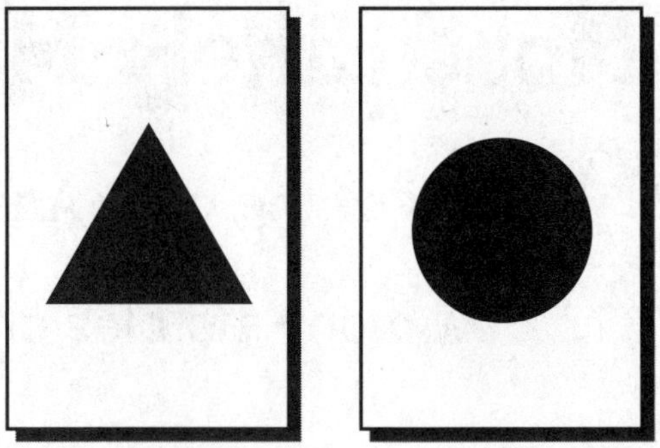

front back

➜ Think about 3 cards. Each card has a ▲ on one side. Each has a ● on the other side. Draw what can happen if you drop them.

1.

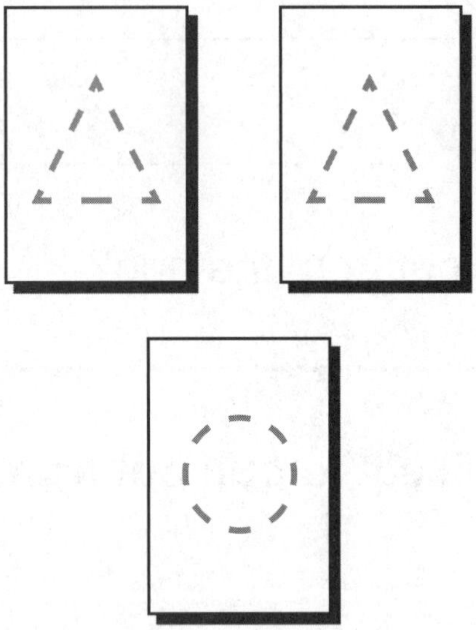

2.

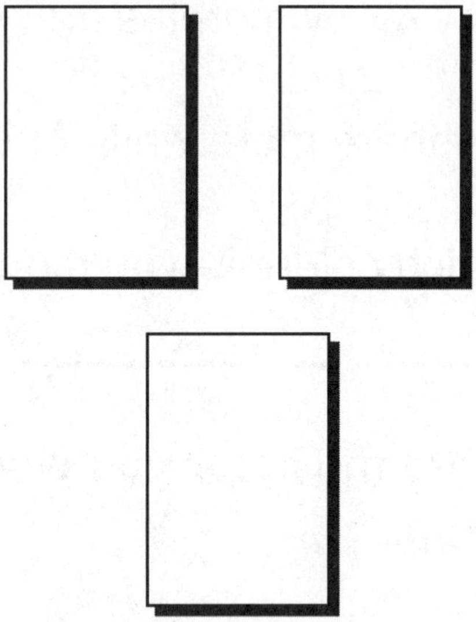

3.

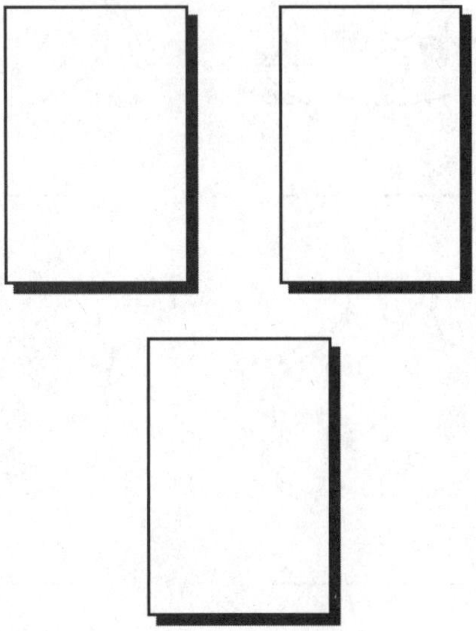

4.

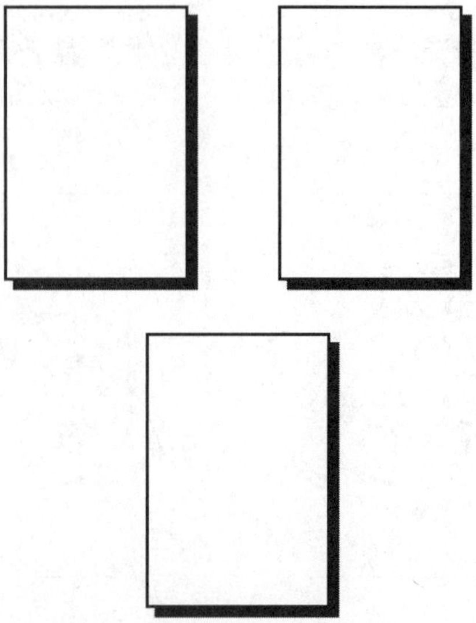

Name ______________________________ Date ________________

INTERPRETING OUTCOMES

It's in the Bag

Work with a partner. Get 7 blue cubes and 3 red cubes. Put them in a bag. Take turns pulling out a cube. Make a tally to show the color. Put the cube back in the bag.

Color	Tally	Total
Blue		
Red		

Answer the questions.

1. What colors could be pulled out from the bag? ________________

____

2. Which color was pulled out more often? ________________

3. Which color was pulled out less often? ________________

4. Why do you think that you pulled out one color more often than the other? ________________________________

____

Name ______________________________ Date ________________

SOLVING WORD PROBLEMS

Take a Guess

Read each story. Solve.

1. The spinner stopped on red 2 times. It stopped on blue 8 times. Draw what you think the spinner looked like. Color your drawing.

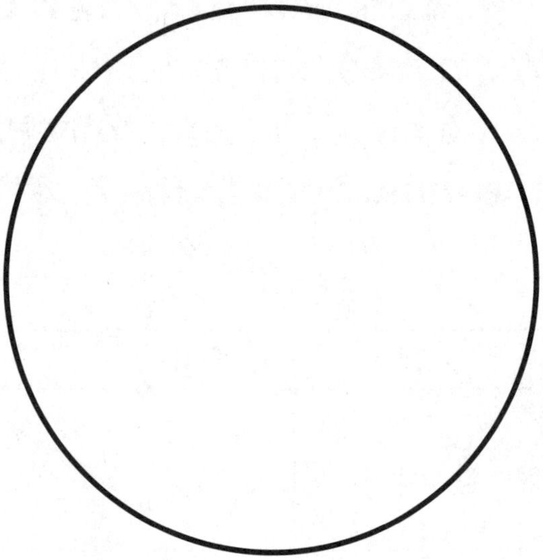

2. Circle the spinner that will more likely stop on black than white.

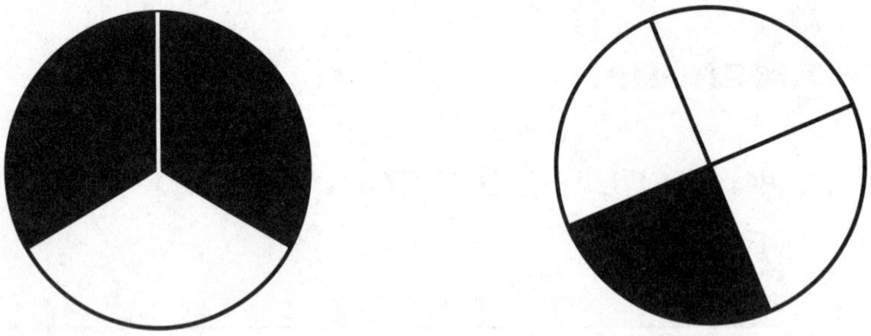

3. Jeff put these cubes in a bag. What color will he most likely pull out? Circle the answer.

white   gray

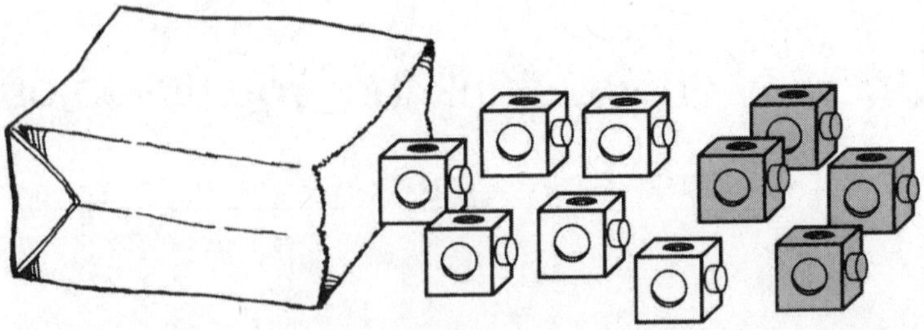

Name ______________________________ Date ______________

Spinning Colors

List all the ways the pointers on the spinners can stop if you play a game that uses both spinners.

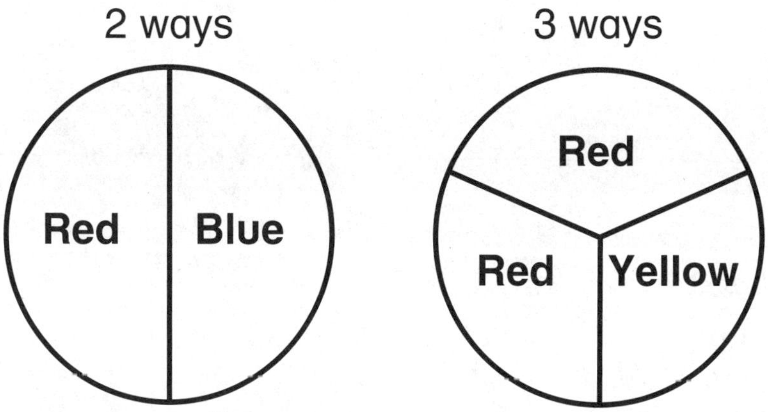

Name ______________________________ Date ______________

Making a Game

Ed wants to make a game. He wants it to be fair. Show 3 ways that Ed can draw the game board so it has 4 equal parts.

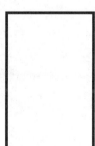

Place-Value Chart

Ones  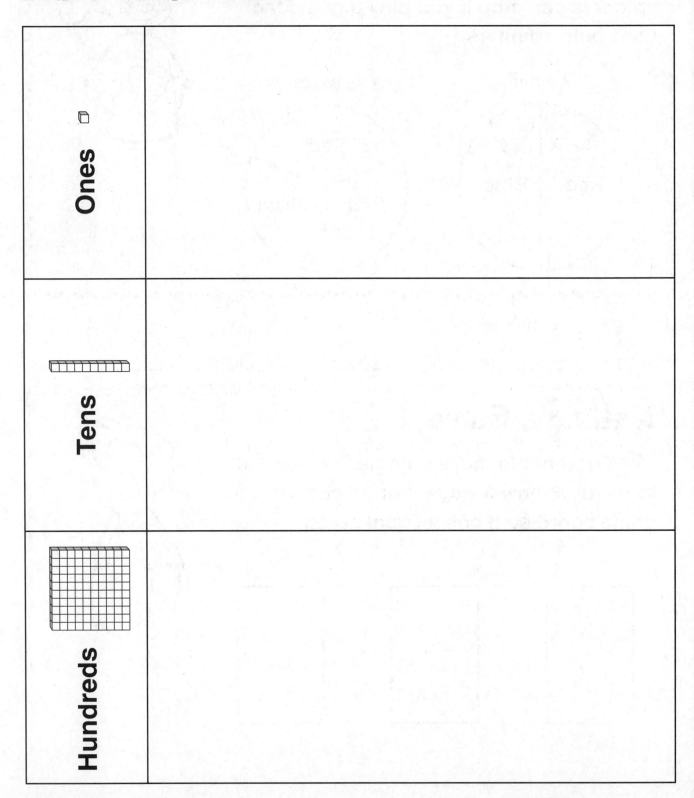	
Tens 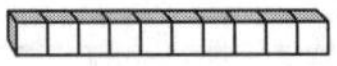	
Hundreds 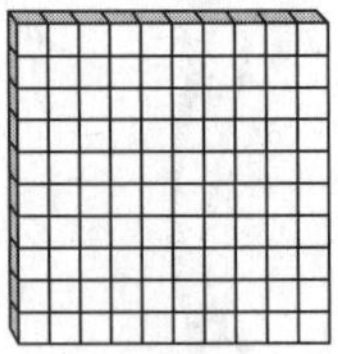	

Analog Clock

Glossary

addend—a number added to another number
addition—joining one thing to another
analog—a clock that uses an hour hand and a minute hand to show the time
bar graph—a graph that uses bars to show how many
bill—paper money
cent—the smallest value of currency in the United States
centimeter—a unit of metric measure for length
checking—using an inverse operation to find if the answer is correct
circle—a round plane figure that has no sides and no corners
coin—metal money
cone—a 3-dimensional figure that has 1 flat face shaped like a circle
congruent—figures that are the same shape and size
corner—the part of a figure where 2 sides meet
cube—a 3-dimensional figure that has a block shape; a single block that represents ones
cylinder—a 3-dimensional figure that has a can shape
difference—the answer when a pair of numbers is subtracted
digital—a clock that uses numbers to show the time
face—the flat side of a figure
fact family—the group of addition and subtraction sentences that use the same three numbers
factor—a number that is multiplied by another number
flat—a manipulative made with 100 joined blocks that represents hundreds
fraction—a way to describe equal parts of a whole or a group
inch—a unit of standard measure for length
line of symmetry—an imaginary line that divides a figure into two parts of the same size and shape
perimeter—the distance around a figure found by adding the lengths of the sides
place value—the value of a digit based on its placement in a number
probability—the chance of an event happening
product—the answer when two or more numbers are multiplied together
pyramid—a 3-dimensional figure that has 4 or 5 flat faces
rectangle—a plane figure that has 4 sides and 4 corners. The opposite sides are the same length.
rectangular prism—a 3-dimensional figure that has a box shape
regrouping—exchanging 10 ones for 1 ten or vice versa
rod—a manipulative made with 10 stacked cubes that represents tens
scale—numbers along the side or bottom of the graph that show how many
side—a straight line
sphere—a 3-dimensional figure that has a ball shape
square—a plane figure that has 4 sides, all of the same length, and 4 corners
subtraction—taking one thing away from another
sum—the answer when two or more numbers are added together
symmetry—having two sides that match exactly
tally—a straight mark made for one thing that is counted
triangle—a plane figure that has 3 sides and 3 corners